The Happiness Secret

'In the early 1960s, it became obvious to me that real happiness didn't lie in material success, adulation or celebrity. I'd experienced them all and they didn't provide for me that elusive, deep-down contentment. Here one of our most gifted Christian communicators spells out what I began to discover for myself all those years ago. Please read. It could well change your life.'

Sir Cliff Richard, OBE

'J.John is one of a kind, and I have a deep respect for him as a speaker, teacher and friend. *The Happiness Secret,* based on the Beatitudes, is truly wonderful. Whether you're outside the church looking in, or whether you already follow Christ, this book will teach you much about the secret to living a happy and blessed life.'

Matt Redman, songwriter

'In a world filled with quick recipes for instant happiness J.John's exploration of the profound teaching of Jesus – which has fascinated the world for two millennia – is filled not only with uncommon honesty but, more than that, with a depth of insight that bears the ring of truth.'

Steve Chalke, MBE
Founder of Oasis Global
UN Special Advisor on Human Trafficking

'J.John and I have been close friends for years. Few people inspire me as he does, whether having a meal with him or listening to him preach. But the people who can write as well as they can preach – or preach as well as they can write – are exceedingly rare. J.John is that rare person. We have written on much the same subjects, but when I read his material I am amazed at how much I have missed. His treatment of the Beatitudes is a perfect example. It reflects a scholar's research, a writer's carefulness, a preacher's passion and a soul-winner's heart. You will be stirred, thrilled and helped by reading this book. It is theologically sound, easy to read, full of wisdom and motivated by the honour and glory of God. I recommend it to the hilt.'

Dr R. T. Kendall
Former minister, Westminster Chapel, London

'J.John is a superb communicator and he is a man who lives out what he teaches. He is always down to earth, humorous and practical.'

Revd Nicky Gumbel
Holy Trinity Brompton, London

'J.John is one of the most creative, influential and respected evangelists in the world today. I have known and admired him for years. If you want to know the real secret of true happiness, you must read this book. With his inimitable style of clarity, conviction, warmth and humour, J.John has taken these "be-attitudes" of Jesus, and translated them in a way that they become guides and realities in the midst of the everyday challenges of life in the twenty-first century.'

Dr Leighton Ford
Charlotte, North Carolina

'J.John has a unique ability and gift to take profound truth and make it comprehensible and accessible to the masses. When I began reading *The Happiness Secret,* my spirit leapt and I found myself not only wishing that I could read faster, but thinking of all the people that I would enthusiastically be giving it to. I am confident that this book will divinely find its way into the lives of many, and that it will clarify and make simple the questions that have haunted the human soul down through the ages.'

Bobbie Houston
Hillsong Church

'In *The Happiness Secret* J.John presents with unparalleled wit and wisdom a manifesto for understanding life, understanding ourselves, and understanding God's will. You are now holding in your hand what will prove to be an abiding masterwork on the embodiment of true biblical happiness – the Beatitudes. Happy reading!'

Dr Tayo Adeyemi
Senior Minister, New Wine Church, London

'This book is compelling. J.John has taken head-on the biggest question of our age – how can I be happy? – and with the intricate application of wisdom, he walks us towards the answer. If only I had known these insights when all my hair was black, I would have saved a fortune on wasted distractions.'

Lord Michael Hastings of Scarisbrick, CBE

Also by J. John

26 Steps to Heaven

The Happiness Secret

J.JOHN

HODDER &
STOUGHTON

First published in Great Britain in 2009 by Hodder & Stoughton
an Hachette UK company

1

A CIP catalogue record for this title is available from the British Library

ISBN 978 0 340 95438 6

Typeset in Adobe Garamond by Ellipsis Books Limited, Glasgow

Printed and bound by Clays Ltd, St Ives plc

Hodder & Stoughton policy is to use papers that are natural,
renewable and recyclable products and made from wood grown in
sustainable forests. The logging and manufacturing processes are expected
to conform to the environmental regulations of the country of origin.

Hodder & Stoughton Ltd
338 Euston Road
London NW1 3BH

www.hodderfaith.com

*I dedicate this book to my unique, adventurous
and eccentric dear friend Canon Andrew White,
who knows about being a peacemaker.
May you and your family truly be blessed.*

Contents

Are You Happy?

There is almost no question more searching than this. Being happy at home, at work and in life generally is the deepest desire of every human being. If we were offered a choice between poverty and happiness and wealth and unhappiness we would all, without hesitating, choose the former.

A recent BBC poll asked whether the government's prime objective should be the 'greatest happiness' or the 'greatest wealth'. A remarkable 81 per cent of those interviewed wanted happiness as the goal. The 'pursuit of happiness' having made it into the United States Declaration of Independence (along with 'life' and 'liberty') as one of the 'unalienable rights' of humankind, happiness is now globally considered to be a key element of any life worth living.

Yet for something so central to human existence, happiness is extraordinarily elusive. What is it exactly? More importantly, how do we find it? In reality, there is nothing more tantalising and more enigmatic than happiness. Chasing happiness is like trying to reach the horizon: it recedes as we get closer. We may sacrifice our money, our career and our health to pursue happiness, but it's like trying to grasp a soap bubble – when we reach out to take hold of it, it suddenly vanishes. In fact, the more we seek happiness the less we are likely to find it. C. P. Snow wrote: 'The pursuit of happiness is a most ridiculous phrase; if you pursue happiness you'll never find it.'

Often we put our hope for happiness in events. 'I will be happy,' we say, 'when I get promotion', or 'when I can retire'. Sometimes we hope for happiness through things: 'I will be happy when I get a new car/computer/house.' Perhaps most of all we hope for happiness through relationships, thinking: 'I will be happy when I get married.' (Is this one of the reasons why so many marriages fail? It's possible to be happily married, but to expect marriage to always make you happy is to put too great a burden on it.)

Events, things, and relationships always short-change us on happiness. They promise but don't deliver. And if you do find happiness, it's hard to keep; it's fragile and short-lived. A chill wind, a sore throat, a traffic jam or a grumpy reception at work can swiftly destroy a happy mood.

Western society continues to seek happiness with an almost manic fervour and increasingly fails to find it. A survey of happiness in the UK suggested that people are much less happy than they were in the 1950s. In 1957 over 50 per cent of those surveyed described themselves as very happy. In 2005, only just over 30 per cent could say the same. Also, in the UK in the ten-year period leading up to 2002, the use of anti-depressants increased by 234 per cent. In 2006 there were 5,556 suicides in adults aged 15 and over in the UK. Another peculiar but disturbing measure of our unhappiness emerged in 2004 when it was revealed that the UK consumption of the anti-depressant Prozac was so great that traces of it could be detected in our rivers and drinking water.

The psychological climate in America is very similar. Americans are desperately searching for happiness but continually coming up short. At the start of 2007, *U.S. News and World Report* dedicated an entire issue to '50 Ways to Improve Your Life in 2007'. The number one suggestion – Get Happy. The article then listed ways to do this – from sipping green tea, to being more grateful, to divorce-proofing your marriage, to enhancing your exercise programme, to redecorating your home. (They suggested starting with getting crown moulding.) In fact, the entire issue was dedicated to ways Americans can find happiness.

The most popular course at Harvard at the moment, with more than 850 enrolees, is called 'How to be happy', and is taught by psychologist Tal Ben-Shahar. There are now Masters programmes throughout the US on how to measure and to achieve happiness. A new one, recently launched at the University of Pennsylvania, focuses on 'positive psychology' – the study of what makes one happy.

The cover of *The Economist* (19 December 2006) read, 'Happiness and how to measure it'. The article highlighted that 'Statistics show that affluent countries have not gotten much happier as they have grown richer. From America to Japan, figures for well-being have not budged.' The article showed that:

> The science of happiness offers two explanations for the paradox. Capitalism it notes, is adept at turning luxuries into necessities – bringing to the masses what elites have always enjoyed. But the flip side of this genius is that people come to take for granted things they once coveted from afar. Frills they never thought they could have are now essentials that they cannot do without. People are stuck on a treadmill: as they achieve a better standard of living, they become inured to its pleasures.

Alexis de Tocqueville expressed this in the nineteenth century, 'So many lucky men restless in the midst of abundance.'

The statistics show that suicide rates continue to rise in the US and that many people suffer from acute sadness and loneliness. Seventy per cent of Americans said their lives consist primarily of acquaintances, and that they had few close friends. People are wealthier, life is busier, and Americans are sad.

This is all very odd when you think that we are three times wealthier than we were in the 1950s. We are also healthier than we have ever been. Most of us should live at least twice as long as Mozart, who died at the age of thirty-four. But although we're healthy and wealthy, we're not happy.

Does this mean we should reject the idea of finding happiness altogether? Some people say it does. Consider this bleak assessment by pre-war American writer Edith Wharton, whose parents are thought to have inspired the phrase 'keeping up with the Joneses':

> There are lots of ways of being miserable, but there's only one way of being comfortable, and that is to stop running round after happiness. If you make up your mind not to be happy there's no reason why you shouldn't have a fairly good time.

According to this view, happiness is an illusion, which is best forgotten. Without more information, we can only guess at how Wharton's parents may have inspired this opinion.

THE INDIRECT PURSUIT OF HAPPINESS

Before you tread down this path of negativity, can I suggest another approach? After all, some things, which we can't capture directly, can be found by indirect means. So, for instance, imagine a man inside a freezing house on a chilly winter's day. He decides to go outside with a big bag to 'catch some heat'. Now, obviously, we all know that would be foolish: you can't 'catch' heat. However, suppose instead that he found some firewood, put *that* in the bag, brought it back and burned it? Then he'd get his heat. What can't be obtained directly can certainly be found by indirect means. I want to suggest that happiness is the same, that we can pursue it indirectly, rather than head-on. This indirect approach won't involve saying, 'If only I had a new . . .' or 'If only such-and-such happened.' It'll involve seeking something altogether different. This mysterious 'something' is a *blessing* and this book is all about how we can be blessed and, therefore, become happy. As the author Matthew Kelly said, 'It is as if God placed this yearning for happiness within each human heart as a spiritual navigation instrument designed to reunite us with our destiny' (Matthew Kelly, *The Rhythm of Life*, Simon & Schuster, 2004).

RELIGIOUS MUMBO-JUMBO?

These are tough times for religious words. On the one hand, we often don't understand what they mean any more. (What is a *benediction* when it's at home?!) On the other hand, some religious words have acquired unjustly negative overtones. If you don't believe me, just try talking to a friend about confession or penance! Strangely enough, though, there are two religious words which have managed to retain a positive image: *blessing* and *blessed*. We may not fully understand what these words mean but people would generally agree that they're gleaming, positive words, even if they are a little old-fashioned.

Take a second or two to think what images the word *blessing* conjures up for you. The happy laughter of family and friends? A warm beach and the sound of waves breaking? Fine food and good music? An endless vista of trees and sunlit fields? You can sense how happiness is related to this concept of being blessed and the great thing is this: unlike happiness, blessing can be sought and found. When it's discovered, it brings life-enhancing peace and happiness and an overflowing, awesome sense of joy.

THE MOST IMPORTANT SERMON OF ALL TIME

The person who knows the route to this blessing is Jesus. As God in human flesh, then resurrected and still living through the Holy Spirit in people today, Jesus has the kind of overview of human problems with which no one can argue. Interestingly, only one of Jesus' full sermons is recorded in the Bible. Traditionally, we have called it the 'Sermon on the Mount', and in it we find Jesus' clues to a life of blessing and happiness.

This sermon, which Jesus' disciple Matthew recorded for us in Chapters 5, 6 and 7 of his Gospel, tells us what Jesus taught in a long series of mysterious statements. In addition to many statements beginning with the word *Blessed*, it is full of many famous sayings of Jesus:

> You are the salt of the earth. But if the salt loses its saltiness, how can it be made salty again? It is no longer good for anything, except to be thrown out and trampled by men. You are the light of the world. A city on a hill cannot be hidden. Neither do people light a lamp and put it under a bowl. Instead they put it on its stand, and it gives light to everyone in the house. In the same way, let your light shine before men, that they may see your good deeds and praise your Father in heaven. (Matthew 5:13–16)

> You have heard that it was said to the people long ago, 'Do not murder, and anyone who murders will be subject to judgment.' But I tell you that anyone who is angry with his brother will be subject to judgment. (Matthew 5:21–22)

> You have heard that it was said, 'Eye for eye, and tooth for tooth.' But I tell you, Do not resist an evil person. If someone strikes you on the right cheek, turn to him the other also. And if

someone wants to sue you and take your tunic, let him have your cloak as well. If someone forces you to go one mile, go with him two miles. (Matthew 5:38–41)

You have heard that it was said, 'Love your neighbour and hate your enemy.' But I tell you: Love your enemies and pray for those who persecute you. (Matthew 5:43–44)

This, then, is how you should pray: 'Our Father in heaven, hallowed be your name, your kingdom come, your will be done on earth as it is in heaven. Give us today our daily bread. Forgive us our debts, as we also have forgiven our debtors. And lead us not into temptation, but deliver us from the evil one.' (Matthew 6:9–14)

Do not store up for yourselves treasures on earth, where moth and rust destroy, and where thieves break in and steal. But store up for yourselves treasures in heaven, where moth and rust do not destroy, and where thieves do not break in and steal. For where your treasure is, there your heart will be also. (Matthew 6:19–21)

Therefore I tell you, do not worry about your life, what you will eat or drink; or about your body, what you will wear. Is not life more important than food, and the body more important than clothes? Look at the birds of the air; they do not sow or reap or store away in barns, and yet your heavenly Father feeds them. Are you not much more valuable than they? Who of you by worrying can add a single hour to his life? (Matthew 6:25–27)

Do not judge, or you too will be judged. For in the same way as you judge others, you will be judged, and with the measure you use, it will be measured to you. (Matthew 7:1–2)

Some of the phrases here ('salt of the earth', 'love your enemies', 'light of the world' and 'treasures in heaven') have become embedded in the English language. However, the Sermon on the Mount is more than a storehouse of fine words: it is insightful teaching on how to live with total delight, joy and freedom. There is so much 'moral high ground' here that it might be better if we called this talk the 'Sermon on the Mountain Range'. You might say that bits of this sermon are found elsewhere in other religions, in particular the Jewish faith of the Old Testament – which is hardly a surprise, given Jesus' background! But as a holistic and succinct expression of how human beings *ought* to live it is without parallel.

Jesus' teachings in this sermon (and elsewhere) are so uncompromising and radical that many people have, through many ingenious attempts, tried to duck them. I touch on this further in the closing chapter and here I just want to say that the most sensible approach is to assume that this sermon really does have relevance to all those who want to follow Jesus throughout all history. The fact that it is so radical a standard is no accident. As Matthew 6:5–8 suggests, Jesus expected His followers to be dramatically different:

> . . . when you pray, do not be like the hypocrites, for they love to pray standing in the synagogues and on the street corners to be seen by men. I tell you the truth, they have received their reward in full. But when you pray, go into your room, close the door and pray to your Father, who is unseen. Then your Father, who sees what is done in secret, will reward you. And when you pray, do not keep on babbling like pagans, for they think they will be heard because of their many words. Do not be like them, for your Father knows what you need before you ask him.

Incidentally, it's hardly worth worrying whether Jesus gave the entire Sermon on the Mount at one go. In reality, Jesus telling illustrative stories, repeating bits and answering questions no doubt extended the teaching. There would have been intervals for prayer, meals and other breaks so the teaching probably went on for several days. We may also safely assume that much of the sermon must have been repeated on other occasions later. What we have in Matthew is, no doubt, the summary version that early Christians probably learned by heart.

MYSTERIOUS STATEMENTS ABOUT BLESSING

If we're interested in discovering the secret of happiness, the statements that Jesus makes at the very beginning of this important sermon must intrigue us. These eight little sayings about what it means to be blessed have come to be known as the 'Beatitudes' (since 'blessed' is *beatus* in Latin). Through the use and repetition of this strange, old-fashioned yet inspiring word 'blessed', Jesus emphasises the importance of what He's saying and makes it memorable. Here then are the statements on which this book is based:

> Blessed are the poor in spirit,
>> for theirs is the kingdom of heaven.
> Blessed are those who mourn,
>> for they will be comforted.
> Blessed are the meek,
>> for they will inherit the earth.
> Blessed are those who hunger and thirst for righteousness,
>> for they will be filled.
> Blessed are the merciful,
>> for they will be shown mercy.
> Blessed are the pure in heart,
>> for they will see God.
> Blessed are the peacemakers,
>> for they will be called sons of God.

Blessed are those who are persecuted because of righteousness,
for theirs is the kingdom of heaven.
(Matthew 5:3–10)

WHAT EXACTLY DOES IT MEAN TO BE BLESSED?

Translators struggle trying to express in English the meaning of
the Greek word *makarios* that Matthew uses. Jesus probably
presented the Beatitudes in the ancient language of Aramaic.
However, we may safely assume that Jesus' first followers knew
what they were doing when they translated His words into Greek.
Some translators, anxious to avoid the peril of religious language,
translate the word in terms of happiness. 'Oh the happiness . . .'
I can understand why this translation is used, but in my opinion
it really doesn't work because, as we've seen, 'happiness' and 'being
blessed' are not the same. Believing they are the same confuses
the concepts of cause and effect, and mistakes the fruit for the
tree. Happiness is a temporary, thin and vulnerable state of mind,
an emotion or feeling. But being blessed is a fixed state, something far more lasting, deep-rooted and permanent. To translate
'blessed' as 'happy' also means that you end up creating rather
nonsensical sentences, such as: 'Happy are you when you mourn.'
Oddly enough, here I am helped by coming from Cyprus, where
the main language is Greek and the island has long been termed
hé makaria or the 'Blessed Isle'. It got its name not because the
islanders believe in God or because He somehow felt favourably
towards it, but because everything that anyone could want – fruit,
wine, fertile soil, good weather – could be found there. To be
blessed then, reflects that idea. It is to have all you really need.

To sum up, then, we might perhaps translate 'blessed' as
'Congratulations!' or 'Good for you!' In this book, I plan to
stick with 'blessed', because although the more upbeat, modern

translations work well with some of the beatitudes, they don't work with all of them. However, when you read such verses as 'blessed are the poor in spirit' remember that what it really means is 'Congratulations', or 'Good for you, you who are poor in Spirit.'

THE HOW, THE WHERE, THE WHEN AND THE WHO

In this book, we'll consider each of the Beatitudes in turn. In each case, we'll focus on the characteristic that Jesus considers blessed, the nature of the blessing promised and finally the relevance for us today. We'll also look at the two verses that follow the eight Beatitudes:

> Blessed are you when people insult you, persecute you and falsely say all kinds of evil against you because of me. Rejoice and be glad, because great is your reward in heaven, for in the same way they persecuted the prophets who were before you. (Matthew 5:11–12)

When we consider each beatitude, I think our priority should not be to debate and analyse. It should be to understand it and live it out. However, before we plunge into the first beatitude it might help if we understand the setting – the where, the when and the who of this sermon:

The *where* is the hill country of Galilee in northern Israel.

The *when* is AD 28–30.

The *who* is Jesus, accompanied by His disciples and the crowds of people who followed them.

Of course, Jesus the man was known during His life as 'Jesus of Nazareth'. At the time when He preached about the Beatitudes, He was a local preacher with a growing reputation for doing and saying remarkable things. In terms of action, His healings, exorcisms and other miracles left little room for questions. Who could challenge His authority when they saw the evidence of His power? In terms of what He said, He was equally remarkable because His words had an extraordinary sharpness and authority.

The disciples Jesus chose for Himself seemed to have been picked more for their ordinariness than anything else. (There's some encouragement for us!) They were already committed to following Jesus, but they were probably already wondering what their leader had up His sleeve. Not only was He unpredictable in the nicest possible way, He also attracted crowds everywhere He went. These 'crowds' did not consist of ordinary people. They were the troubled people of society, who were probably already edging in quietly around the semicircle of the disciples. These people were social outcasts, socially 'challenged' or at best disadvantaged in terms of political hierarchies and opportunities. They were trapped between the jaws of a double oppression. On the one hand there was the brutality of the 'your-money-or-your-life' thuggery of Roman occupation. On the other, they inevitably must have suffered from the heavy-handed, intrusive 'you-must-do-this-or-else' religion of the Pharisees. It was in this context that Jesus gave this teaching.

A WORD OF WARNING

Before we go on, let me issue what may seem to be an odd warning. The one really wrong thing you can do with these statements is treat them as 'religious' or 'spiritual' sayings. They're not like the words some fresh-faced choristers might sing in a candle-lit cathedral. They're also nothing like the beautifully written gold lettering on a piece of parchment, which you might come across on a boring museum tour. They're not even like something that might be part of some ancient incantation.

If you're under the illusion that the Beatitudes are like any of these, you're missing the point. Seeing them in the same light as other religious words or phrases would drain them of their contemporary relevance. No, these sayings are far more practical than that. They're a 'how to' for living in the real world, full of the powers, frustrations, and pressures that we all know so well. They relate to people who are too busy for spiritual things, or who are suffering at the hands of others who despise anything vaguely religious. They speak straight to the heart of people who are dealing with the consequences of a life lived alongside individuals whose last priority is to give honour to God. Jesus knew how tough the real world was – let's not forget His experience of it, in His life and death.

In any case, if you take a close look at the Beatitudes you'll soon see that they're very unlike conventional religious or spiritual sayings. They're nothing like the snappy, feel-good soundbites you find in upbeat church services and they're a long way from the bland platitudes you find in birthday cards and calendars. Actually, they're utterly and stunningly radical. Take the third one, for example: 'Blessed are the meek, for they will inherit the earth.' We haven't even begun to understand what this means unless we shake our head and mutter, 'No way!' or even 'Pull the other leg!' The other beatitudes are just as shocking if we really absorb them. They all go completely against the grain and fly in the face of popular wisdom. They're not *remotely* natural or intuitive. In fact, they're so unnatural, they're either completely illogical and useless – or they are an inspiration for a different kind of life.

Finally, let's remember that although each beatitude relates to a challenging life experience, every beatitude talks about a *blessing*, not a curse of any kind. So many people are put off by religion and they're wary of anything that involves any mention of God or Jesus. It's as if these words are a blight on the human race! They feel sure that whenever they open the Bible they will be condemned. Christianity is some great black thundercloud of judgement hovering above that will, at best, unleash a torrent of rain on them, and at worst, bolts of lightning.

Notice that Matthew sets the Beatitudes right at the very beginning in his account of Jesus' teaching. This is no accident. These statements constitute the distilled essence of what Jesus taught about how to live a truly human, happy and *blessed* life. Not surprising, then, that these statements hold the key to the secret of happiness.

It is my hope that what I have written in this book will help you along the road to blessing. I have confidence that it will, not because it is based on my thoughts and wisdom, but because it is based on the teaching of Jesus, who, more than any other human being, has the best claim to know about blessing and to speak of it reliably. For Jesus was nothing less than God on earth who said, 'I have come that their joy may be complete.'

1

Be Poor in Spirit

Blessed are the poor in spirit,
for theirs is the kingdom of heaven.
(Matthew 5:3)

As we have seen in the introduction, Jesus starts His sermon by saying, 'Blessed are the poor in spirit, for theirs is the kingdom of heaven.' 'Blessed' means 'Congratulations!' or, as the Australians would say, 'Good on you!' This term blessed also means 'Oh the bliss'. It suggests utter delight and joy. So Jesus says here that we should congratulate the 'poor in spirit' as the people who will experience bliss in this life. At first glance this doesn't seem to make much sense. The world tells us that power, money and relationships will bring us happiness. However, Jesus, the greatest teacher on the key to life, says that we need to celebrate and congratulate those who are poor in spirit. What is He on about?

There are three possible ways to interpret the phrase 'poor in spirit'.

It could mean being *spiritually impoverished*. This interpretation reminds us that when we come to God, we can only plead for mercy and grace because we have no other basis upon which to stand – we're just so imperfect.

It could simply mean *discouraged*. According to this view, it is only when we are completely humbled by our circumstances that we are in the right frame of mind to approach God. Some argue that we only begin to seek God when we have hit rock bottom in our lives.

Some people think the odd phrase 'poor in spirit' could refer not to spiritual poverty, but to *real-world financial poverty*. According to this view it is the oppressed – those without wealth – who are blessed. Actually, I disagree with this interpretation, although being materially poor may enable people to be more receptive to God. And this would describe the material condition of Matthew's readers both in economically depressed Galilee, and after the destruction of Jerusalem.

I think the best meaning of the statement 'Blessed are the poor in spirit' is that those who find blessing (and ultimately, happiness) are those who recognise that they are *spiritually bankrupt*. This meaning relates to the first and second of the possible interpretations given above. In other words, the people who are blessed are the ones who have recognised that they are wholly dependent on God. The poor are those who, for whatever reason, recognise their dire need of the grace of God.

In the first beatitude, 'blessed are the poor in spirit', Jesus lays the foundation stone of His teaching. He is setting out the only basis on which we can relate to God, the only way in which we can be blessed and the only way in which we can experience lasting happiness. It is by depending on God and acknowledging our need for God that we can experience God's blessing.

If we're perfectly honest, we might find this rather annoying. We like to think we're the good guys. We like to think we've achieved something, that all our good efforts count, and that God is somehow impressed by what we've done – that we are self-sufficient, relying on our salary, investments and savings, or even our social standing. But Jesus' teaching here challenges that idea, because He's reminding us that our credit rating with the only bank that really matters is not at all good. The path to blessing (and to happiness) must begin with the stark recognition that we're all heavily in debt. It may be incredibly hard to accept, but it is the person who recognises the enormity of their debt to God, so becoming poor in spirit, who will be blessed.

One reason why we may have difficulty accepting Jesus' statement is because it flies in the face of contemporary culture. Modern, Western culture puts the emphasis *not* on admitting how much we're in debt spiritually, psychologically or materially, but on affirming how much we're in credit. A library of literature declares that the only way to live is to have a positive attitude of self-affirmation: *Believe in yourself! Be the master of your own destiny! Dare to affirm who you are! Transform yourself!* It's not surprising, then, that we might feel uncomfortable about the foundation stone that Jesus put in place. Instead of saying we can pull ourselves up by our bootstraps, Jesus is saying that we become blessed when we recognise we need help – when we acknowledge that we are spiritually poor.

You know those jokes that begin, 'How many plumbers/vicars/psychiatrists does it take to change a light bulb?' Some of the most amusing are the ones where the answer is something along the lines of 'None! They think the light bulb is just fine as it is.' This reminds us of the crux of the issue: until we admit there's a problem, i.e. that we need help, we can't possibly make any progress. Just as no amount of denial or wishful thinking will fix a failed light bulb, so no amount of introspection or repeatedly chanted mantras will fix our lives.

If you still have difficulty accepting this, consider what it's like dealing with a friend or relative who is anorexic, or who has an alcohol problem. If you've struggled with this yourself, you'll know that the first and indispensable step is for them to recognise that a problem exists in the first place. Anything else is denial and leads to non-action, deceit, or at best a lack of commitment to any action that is taken. And it isn't just with anorexia or alcohol abuse that this denial occurs. Ask the spouse of a hopeless car navigator and you may hear them say, 'The trouble is, they'll never admit they're lost.' The same phenomenon occurs in other areas of life. There are DIY plumbers who flood a succession of houses, sailors who end up being repeatedly rescued by the lifeboat service and any number of reckless computer 'experts' who reconfigure their computers and yet again lose all their files! They have all failed to learn that sometimes the greatest wisdom lies in admitting that you can't do whatever it is you want to do. In the same way, admitting that you're poor in spirit involves acknowledging that you need help. It's worth doing simply because it's likely to lead to satisfaction and happiness. We could actually paraphrase this beatitude and accurately say: 'People who are spiritually, socially and materially self-sufficient will be unhappy', for these are the very people who are not acknowledging their own inadequacy and their need for God.

Ironically enough, there's one particular type of person who finds the idea of admitting spiritual poverty particularly difficult to accept – the religious type. Those who've spent their whole lives trying to build up credit with God don't take kindly to being told the currency they've invested in so heavily is actually worthless, or that the coins they've been saving actually amount to very little. The point is that God befriends those who are prepared to confess to being bankrupt, not those who gloat over their savings.

Another group of people, on the other hand, find this teaching much easier to accept: people who are moral failures and who have come to the end of their resources, i.e. the very people we frown upon, the ones we think have utterly blown it in the area of right and wrong. So it's no wonder that in His lifetime Jesus won the trust and affection of people whose lives were moral disaster areas – prostitutes and tax collectors who collaborated with the enemy, the Romans. It's no wonder Jesus fell foul of the self-righteous to the extent that they arranged for Him to be executed on trumped-up charges. Nothing much has changed. But the fact remains that heaven only admits people who know they've utterly failed to meet the entrance requirements. God is ready and waiting to accept and embrace all those who come to Him in poverty.

Why does God do this? Why does He make the only way to Him the one that requires us to be beggars? Is He some kind of bully who delights in seeing us stand before Him squirming and muttering, 'Sorry God, I guess I really messed up'? It's possible to understand how He's not at all like this if we imagine suddenly being lumbered with some appalling bill for a million pounds. Clearly, swaggering up to our creditor with a cheque for £50 is not going to help in the least – in fact, it's going to be counter-productive because it's likely to throw our creditor into a rage. The sad fact is that we all have that enormous bill to pay – because whether we're saints or sinners in the world's eyes, we are all debtors before the perfect and holy God. None of us live according to the perfect standard of God. We need to accept that God is willing to 'let us off' completely if we'll only acknowledge the enormous debt we've built up through our wrongdoing and wrong attitudes.

ON WEALTH AND POVERTY

Now what about financial wealth? Is Jesus against riches? Frankly, the easiest answer would be to say that Jesus talked about the 'poor in *spirit*' and that therefore this has nothing to do with financial wealth.

Although this may well be the easiest answer, it probably isn't the most honest. For one thing, Luke's Gospel has a version of the Beatitudes (delivered at another time and place) that simply states, 'Blessed are you who are poor' (Luke 6:20), omitting Matthew's more specific focus. And there are other favourable comments towards the poor in the Gospels. So is Jesus also commending people who are financially broke or literally impoverished? I don't think so, for several reasons.

In Jesus' day the main issue didn't seem to be wealth itself, but people's attitude towards it. The general view was to see riches as a reward from God for living well. In other words, the rich viewed their wealth as a sign that God approved of their lifestyle: being wealthy proved you were godly. Of course, such a viewpoint also had implications with regard to poverty. Poverty was also God's public verdict, so being penniless was apparently a sign that someone had behaved badly. It was a neat, simple equation: goodness brings wealth, bad behaviour and rebellion bring poverty. It was also a very harmful philosophy because it resulted in a wealthy elite feeling smug and complacent about a poverty-stricken underclass who were depressed and guilty. Jesus completely dismantles this prevalent view of wealth and poverty.

Jesus' teaching is, oddly enough, harshest on the rich. After all, if the only way to heaven is by pleading your spiritual bankruptcy, then taking your prosperity as a sign from God that you are OK fatally blinds you to your desperate need of Him. It's no wonder that Jesus could announce that it was the poor – and the poor in spirit – who would be blessed.

Even if we don't hold to this extreme view of the significance of riches, wealth still blinds people today. First, it blinds men and women by giving them the illusion of power and security in an uncertain world, which in turn gives them a fatal sense of self-sufficiency. Second, it blinds people by distracting them from their eternal destiny. The pleasures and cares that come with wealth may push thoughts of God and heaven away. The poor, meanwhile, have limited access to worldly goods and are more prone to rely on God for mercy and provision. Finally, wealth can make men and women blind to the need to care for others by making them think their wealth gives them a right to rule over others. From all points of view, then, wealth needs a health warning!

Suggesting the need to be wary of wealth does not mean we need to conclude that financial poverty is a blessing. That would be naïve, because poverty is certainly not part of God's plan for the world. We know that Jesus' followers included the rich because Paul, writing to the Corinthian church, mentions that some believers there were wealthy. Throughout the Bible, however, God is very clear that the rich are to share their wealth with those who have need. In the Old Testament, Jews are told to leave a portion of their harvest for the poor and the stranger. They are obligated to give alms to the poor. Furthermore, in the New Testament, Jesus says clearly that care for the poor is synonymous with caring for God Himself. Jesus calls on all believers to be His love in the world.

Jesus says,

But when the Son of Man comes in his glory, and all the angels with him, then he will sit upon his glorious throne. All the nations will be gathered in his presence, and he will separate the people as a shepherd separates the sheep from the goats. He will place the sheep at his right hand and the goats at his left.

Then the King will say to those on his right, 'Come, you who are blessed by my Father, inherit the Kingdom prepared for you from the creation of the world. For I was hungry, and you fed me. I was thirsty, and you gave me a drink. I was a stranger, and you invited me into your home. I was naked, and you gave me clothing. I was sick, and you cared for me. I was in prison, and you visited me.'

Then these righteous ones will reply, 'Lord, when did we ever see you hungry and feed you? Or thirsty and give you something to drink? Or a stranger and show you hospitality? Or naked and give you clothing? When did we ever see you sick or in prison and visit you?'

And the King will say, 'I tell you the truth, when you did it to one of the least of these my brothers and sisters, you were doing it to me!'

Then the King will turn to those on the left and say, 'Away with you, you cursed ones, into the eternal fire prepared for the devil and his demons. For I was hungry, and you didn't feed me. I was thirsty, and you didn't give me a drink. I was a stranger, and you didn't invite me into your home. I was naked, and you didn't give me clothing. I was sick and in prison, and you didn't visit me.'

Then they will reply, 'Lord, when did we ever see you hungry or thirsty or a stranger or naked or sick or in prison, and not help you?'

And he will answer, 'I tell you the truth, when you refused to help the least of these my brothers and sisters, you were refusing to help me.'

And they will go away into eternal punishment, but the righteous will go into eternal life. (Matthew 25:31–46, NLT)

As St Teresa of Avila said, 'We are the hands and feet of Jesus.' We are all called to share and give to others on behalf of God.

THE POINT

The most important aspect to remember about the first beatitude is that a life of happiness begins when we come to God and admit our need for Him. We must accept that the only way to have a relationship with God is not by building ourselves up before Him, but by pleading utter defeat. Most religions advocate that the way to God is by following a set of rules. The world tells us the way to God is by having it all together and succeeding in areas of power and wealth. Jesus says the way to Him is by admitting our need for Him and accepting His love. He says, 'Come to me, all of you who are weary and carry heavy burdens, and I will give you rest' (Matthew 11:28, NLT). He says, 'Look! I stand at the door and knock. If you hear my voice and open the door, I will come in, and we will share a meal together as friends' (Revelation 3:20, NLT).

This teaching is repeated elsewhere in the New Testament, sometimes using the language of 'guilt', rather than poverty. The apostle Paul says: 'For everyone has sinned; we all fall short of God's glorious standard' (Romans 3:23, NLT). In the next sentence though, he presents the answer to our inadequacy before God. 'Yet God, with undeserved kindness, declares that we are righteous. He did this through Christ Jesus when he freed us from the penalty for our sins. For God presented Jesus as the sacrifice for sin. People are made right with God when they believe that Jesus sacrificed his life, shedding his blood' (Romans 3:24–25, NLT). In other words, to those who admit their poverty, God gives the wealth and riches of His own Son. The good news is that true happiness, salvation and relationship with God are made available to all humanity through Jesus Christ. The name Jesus actually means 'God to the rescue'. When we come to Jesus covered in the muck and poverty of our lives, He wraps us in a clean glistening white robe of forgiveness.

THE BLESSING OF GAINING
THE KINGDOM OF HEAVEN

At the end of this and the last (eighth) beatitude, Jesus says the kingdom of heaven belongs to the poor in spirit. But what exactly is this 'kingdom of heaven'? The first thing to note is that the 'kingdom of heaven' is exactly the same as the 'kingdom of God' mentioned elsewhere in the Gospels. Then, as now, Jews preferred to avoid using the word 'God' and so used an alternative such as 'heaven'. Second, we need to understand that the kingdom Jesus talks about is not an isolated geographical place, but *anywhere* God is in charge, where God rules through Christ. Finally, we need to remember that although it is not a specific place at the moment, one day it will be *all places*.

So how should we understand the kingdom? Consider this illustration. A couple are sent from their much-loved home country to some far-off and much less developed land. Inevitably, they see themselves as representing their old country while they're living abroad. Therefore, they're careful to set a good example and although they prosper, they never forget the land they came from, which they eventually plan to return to. They long for their home-land, use its language together, celebrate its festivals and hang pictures of it on their walls. The result is that while they are good citizens of their new country, their ultimate allegiance and hope lies with this other, far-off land. To belong to the kingdom of God is like this. It is to have another citizenship, to live by other rules and to look forward to going to a better place.

Yet the kingdom of heaven is more than some distant future destination because people inhabiting this world are already experiencing it. In the Gospel of John, Jesus says that eternal life begins now. This means that while we are here on earth we can experience a joyful, blissful life with Jesus. This does not mean we will not have troubles. Jesus said, 'In this world you will have trouble. But take heart! I have overcome the world' (John 16:33). Jesus is highlighting the reality that life in relationship with Him brings much joy, no matter what the circumstances. People who experience it may be elderly, frail or poor, but they quietly breathe the kingdom's air, often unnoticed by those who bustle busily past them. Those who live in the light of heaven rejoice in its distant music and wait, hoping that death will take them across that thin boundary between the present and the future of God's kingdom.

TO SUM UP

In case you still find yourself questioning this first beatitude, let's summarise what it means to say that we're blessed if we're poor in spirit.

It means that spiritual poverty provides the *only* basis for a relationship with God. Jesus is pointing out here that in order to make contact with God we must first *admit* our need. It seems fair – after all, drowning swimmers don't negotiate with the captain of the lifeboat. They cry out for help.

Being 'poor in spirit' means we become totally dependent on God in every area of our life. It's as if Jesus is saying we're like patients in a 'high dependency unit' whose very survival depends on all those wires, tubes and respirator pipes. It would be utter madness to start throwing away the very links that keep us alive. We need to be dependent on God.

Being 'poor in spirit' *allows* God to work in our lives. I believe that one of the main reasons why God does not do great things through us is that we are too quick to claim credit. Our own pride and our tendency to search for our own glory means that we get in the way. The only partnership with Him that can work is one where He is firmly in charge.

Being 'poor in spirit' is the best basis for prayer – for communication with God. While most of us recognise that prayer is vital, most of us find it very hard. I suggest that one reason for this is because we don't really have the poverty of spirit that drives us to prayer. Imagine working in an office where there is a senior manager with whom you don't work directly. Perhaps you meet this man or woman a couple of times a week in the cafeteria, and you always exchange a few words. However, there's no depth to your relationship. Then suddenly, he or she becomes appointed as your boss on some difficult project. Things change and your once insignificant relationship is now transformed. You're constantly in touch and you listen carefully to what this person says. Equally, you now think hard about what you're going to say to them: how will you represent yourself or your position? How will you ask them for the resources you need to do the job? Now the reason why the relationship has changed is quite simple: you are now dependent on this person. It seems to me we need something of that attitude in prayer. We do not come before God as equals around the table; we come as people who are utterly, totally dependent on God – totally *poor* in spirit. Recognising this will inevitably revolutionise the way we pray.

Being 'poor in spirit' makes it impossible for us to be proud or arrogant, both of which are terribly corrupting. Have you realised how vulnerable proud people are? Their image is so important that they'll often make wrong decisions or deny something they know to be true, simply in order to save face! About the only way to get them to do anything right is to make them think it was their idea in the first place. Since they are so concerned about 'being right', arrogant and proud people tend to surround themselves with the sort of advisers who will always agree with them and never contradict anything they say. That, of course, is lethal, as we've seen throughout history. How many times have leaders plunged entire nations into utterly disastrous and bloody wars, simply because of their pride? And on a smaller scale, how many organisations – and families – have been wrecked because of a single person's arrogance?

In summary, then, being poor in spirit means adopting a mindset that is far from arrogant. It means evaluating our own worth truthfully and honestly. The outcome, inevitably, is improved relationships, because for any relationship to be successful, the individuals involved need to accept their vulnerability and need for grace. When people are 'poor in spirit' nobody can feel superior so the playing field becomes even. Do you see how being 'poor in spirit' is not just a religious curiosity, but also the very foundation of a blessed life?

2

Be Mournful!

Blessed are those who mourn,
for they will be comforted.
(Matthew 5:4)

WHY READ THIS?

You may have just read the word 'mourn' and decided that you really don't like the sound of what's coming. The very word carries such negative baggage (all that suffering, grief and sadness) that you may feel like skipping this chapter altogether. Let me give you four reasons why you shouldn't fast forward.

This is one of the primary keys to living a happy life

As I said in the introduction, there's a logical development to the Beatitudes that we need to follow. We can't pick and mix the Beatitudes any more than we can skip chapters in a novel. If we miss what this statement means, we won't have a true under-standing of the sequence of the Beatitudes and their progression. We don't want to miss out on the author of life's advice on great living in this world and beyond. Jesus doesn't want us just to survive, he wants us to thrive.

This is not just about death

The grief that Jesus is talking about is not simply the emotion of bereavement. Here, Jesus is touching on a range of very different types of suffering, all of which are part of the human experience. He's talking about the sadness we might feel about our own inadequacies, or regret concerning the mistakes we have made and the people we have hurt, as well as the discouragement or even depression we experience when we hear about other people's situations both close to us and in the world in general.

We're all in mourning and Jesus wants to help!

We're bound to be in mourning ourselves at many points in our lives. Our society often shuns negative emotions – however, it is necessary to deal with them. Events such as unemployment, disease and depression inevitably occur, and no amount of wishing them away will alter their reality. However much we prefer not to talk about dentists we all know we need them. Imagine someone who is so negative about the idea of dentists that they decide they will never go to one. Far from making the problem go away, this will ensure that, one day, they have such catastrophic dental problems that they will have to undergo some pretty traumatic treatment. Facing up to going to the dentist now may actually mean that in the future they have fewer really painful dental appointments. Such is the case with painful emotions and events. The sooner we face them, the better off we will be in the long run. Above all, Jesus promises we will be blessed as we release grief and experience His comfort. Denial results in so much garbage being buried in our lives. It will continue to fester and become toxic.

There's something in it for us

There are actually huge benefits to be gained from mourning, both alone and alongside others. Instead of seeing our own or other people's sadness as 'uncool', 'embarrassing' or tantamount to being a wet blanket, we need to recognise the support we can give and receive if we allow grief to be expressed. In modern Western culture, the fact that we don't go out of our way to help people who are mourning makes the grief all the harder to bear, because bereaved people feel totally isolated. Grief has become a disease that nobody wants to 'catch'! If you are secretly mourning alone right now, you'll know how good it would feel to have someone mourning alongside you – listening to you or just being there for you, in whatever way you needed. If as you read this you're thinking of someone *else* who's mourning, think how much you might be able to help that person by making contact. Even though sharing other people's grief inevitably involves risk, just as any commitment does, it is well worth it. As we draw closer to people and their real feelings, we develop deeper, richer relationships and experience the benefits of being more strongly committed to people. The end result of helping others in their pain is a whole lot of good feelings! We really can take on board Paul's advice to the church in Rome to 'rejoice with those who rejoice; mourn with those who mourn' (Romans 12:15). And we can believe Jesus' own statement: 'Blessed are those who mourn', as we will see in this chapter. We have to learn to work through our grief in order to find eventual release.

The promise of receiving God's comfort

The night before Jesus was betrayed He promised that He would not abandon His followers but He would send an Advocate, the Holy Spirit, who would comfort, guide, and fill His followers

(John 14). Jesus said, 'I will not leave you as orphans; I will come to you' (John 14:18). Jesus promises that He will never leave us nor forsake us (Hebrews 13:5). He promises that He will be with us even to the end of the age (Matthew 28). When going through struggles we can hold fast to Jesus' promise of the comfort of His Holy Spirit. This is the most powerful comfort – beyond any human understanding. He promises to give the same Spirit that raised Jesus from the dead to every believer. When we mourn, Jesus promises that the great comforter, the Holy Spirit, will minister to us. This is why, time and again, we see people going through the worst kinds of pain with an unexplainable peace and joy. This is why we see people suffering and praising God simultaneously. The great Christian paradox is that when we are weak, He is strong. When His strength comes to comfort us, we then experience a peace that surpasses human understanding. It is a wonderful gift from God.

So carry on reading, please! Denial is not going to get you anywhere, but recognition of your true feelings and commitment to support others and to receive Jesus' profound comfort results in real bliss.

WHAT DOES IT MEAN TO 'MOURN' SOMETHING?

We have many different verbs to talk about experiencing sorrow. We talk about grieving, feeling sad, feeling miserable, weeping, lamenting, feeling down in the dumps, being upset, feeling blue, out of sorts or depressed – the list goes on! The Ancient Greeks also had numerous ways of talking about grief but the word used in the Beatitudes indicates a very serious state of affairs. It suggests the type of mourning and weeping you might find at a funeral or in a deep state of depression. In an Eastern culture grief is openly expressed rather than bottled up. A stiff-upper-lip attitude can lead to emotional lockjaw!

From this we can tell that Jesus' statement is about comforting people who are bereaved, deeply unhappy or in despair. It's likely that Jesus is focusing both on people who are experiencing sadness as a result of *external* events or circumstances such as death, poverty or injustice and on people who struggle with *internally* focused grief. This second group of people might be unhappy about the state of their lives, and experience a general sense of unease and sadness such as depression, mental illness or low self-esteem.

THE SHADOWY SIDE OF LIFE

You probably know several and possibly *many* people who suffer from some sort of mental darkness. It is also likely that you have experienced some negative emotions yourself. Statistics make this very clear, as we began to see in the introduction. The recent rise in anti-depressant drug use means that in 2006 more than 31 million prescriptions for drugs such as Prozac were issued in the UK (to an adult population of around 48 million). (Of course repeat prescriptions brings down the overall percentage of the population on anti depressants, but it is still significantly high.) Given that many who suffer under the shadowy side of life do not seek pharmaceutical help, the true number of those whose lives are far from happy must be enormous. And, as noted before, the number of suicides is also truly sobering. The fact that over 5,000 people kill themselves each year in the UK alone, and the fact that still more people attempt suicide, means the situation is serious. If we understand the word 'mourn' to refer to those who currently find life emotionally painful or unbearable, then we're talking about huge numbers of people facing an incredible amount of suffering.

If you doubt these statistics, remember that there's a certain amount of inevitability to this kind of mourning. After all, people are bound to experience at least some form of misery in their lives over the course of a lifetime. Isn't it an unusual person who hasn't, at least briefly, felt that 'life sucks'? Mourning, or, as we usually define it, bereavement, is a case in point. You either live long enough to be subjected to mourning or you die young enough to become the subject of it. Even putting death aside, there are other factors such as disease, unemployment and major disappointments or catastrophes in life. So we clearly can't opt out of sorrow and loss altogether and switch from 'black' to 'white' – the greyness of life is inevitable from time to time. No one, not even the luckiest or the richest among us, can avoid periods of disappointment and pain.

In this respect it's interesting to consider why we all like to think we're happy. When people ask us how we are, our automatic response is usually to give a breezy, 'Fine, thanks!' Although few people expose themselves to ridicule by proclaiming they're happy to anyone who will listen, we certainly do all prefer to *believe* that we're happy really. Is this why we constantly try to give the impression we're not only happy, but also healthy, wealthy and sexually fulfilled? And perhaps we also need to consider why we all seem to prefer to believe that in reality we're immortal. Constantly – through cosmetics, clothes, plastic surgery and exercise – we try to maintain or attain a youthful physical appearance. Sadly, we must accept that the reality is actually very, very different. Although Thomas Hobbes may have been overly filled with doom and gloom when he said in 1651 that life is 'solitary, poor, nasty, brutish and short', the modern opposite – that life is some kind of everlasting, fun-filled party – is equally dangerous, unrealistic and simply untrue.

Does this surprise you? As a Christian aren't I supposed to believe in a God who is loving and in a Holy Spirit who brings along – among other things – joy? I am supposed to believe that and I do – but I also recognise that there is evil in the world and that things are not as God first intended them to be. Sorrow, illness and death were not part of God's original plan. To use the theological phrase, this is an 'alienated universe' (Genesis 3) contaminated by evil. It is true that one day, evil will end and the universe will be remade so that it contains only goodness – but in the meantime we must cope with the world being more like a battlefield than a playground. However, we must remember that no matter how traumatic the battlefield, we live in hope because of Jesus.

MOURNING OUR OWN INADEQUACIES

As well as living in a messed-up world, we must also cope with the fact that we ourselves are messed up and fall terribly short of God's standards. This results in suffering which is essentially self-inflicted. In this second beatitude, Jesus included the type of mourning that results from an awareness of our own ingrained sinful nature. He included people who seriously understand the implications of their failure, and the failure of others, before God.

We can see how this second beatitude follows on from the first one if we remember that the first one implied that we need to mentally acknowledge that we are debtors to God. In order to do this on an emotional level, we need to feel the impact of being in debt to God. In other words, if the first beatitude referred to head knowledge, this second one refers to our heart's reaction.

The good news of this beatitude is that here Jesus makes clear that mourning our own sinfulness makes us blessed. Although it might be difficult to admit to our own weakness in this respect, we can be happy that being a sinner who *mourns* the reality of our sin makes us deeply loved and valued in God's sight. While modern upbeat paraphrases such as 'negative personality traits', 'bad genes' and 'disordered personality' might make us socially acceptable in some kind of warped way, or might make us sound 'curable', given a few convenient medical advances, recognising the raw, old-fashioned truth behind the word 'sinner' makes us right with God. The thought of garnering happiness and acceptance via the acknowledgement of sin in our lives is unsettling, but that's the way we must go. Unless we get sin out of the way early on along the path to God, it will burden us for the rest of the journey. While problems like a 'disordered personality' or 'tainted genes' might theoretically be curable in the future, sin can be treated both instantly and permanently, with virtually no technology or specialist treatment!

Obviously, this beatitude is very close to the great biblical theme of repentance (meaning turning away from our sin to God for forgiveness). Let me make three observations before we move on.

Mourning over sin is no bizarre, morbid fad of the modern Christian evangelical movement. Since the beginning of God's interaction with humanity, people have grieved their sins. Some 460 years ago the Anglican Church – to which I am happy to belong – defined its beliefs in the *Book of Common Prayer*. In it, Archbishop Cranmer wrote the following prayer for use just before Holy Communion: 'We acknowledge and bewail our manifold sins and wickedness, which we from time to time most grievously have committed, by thought, word and deed, against thy divine majesty, provoking most justly thy wrath and indignation against us.' That certainly is taking spiritual mourning seriously – and it was already being done almost five centuries ago!

The kind of mourning we're talking about here is *purposeful*. It's not some non-specific lamenting on the lines of 'Oh, how wretched I am!' That kind of sentiment can lead to feelings of morbid worthlessness; it is not of God, and we need to avoid it. The purposefulness of the mourning comes from the fact that instead of focusing on the disease, it focuses on the cure. It constitutes a focused recognition of what we have done wrong and a desire for God to forgive us. In other words, rather than focusing on a wound to the point where it becomes an open sore, our focus is on allowing it to heal altogether. In practical terms this may mean praying: 'Lord, I'm sorry for the angry way I spoke to Ellen yesterday. Forgive me for my hasty tongue,' or 'Lord, I recognise I pushed people around at the meeting this morning. Forgive me for my pride.' You get the idea? It's a question of being specific and genuinely wanting to receive forgiveness. And it will inevitably involve taking appropriate action too – for instance apologising to Ellen, or making an effort to behave more considerately at the next meeting.

We're talking about *confident* mourning. From the Bible we know that if we put our trust in Christ our sins will be forgiven. Bible-based Christianity knows nothing of the sort of wishful religious thinking where the best that exists is a vague hope that God will forgive what we have done wrong. We understand that the death of Jesus on the cross is God's personal and permanent answer to sin, so we have confidence that our own sin has been dealt with. As St Peter said in 1 Peter 3:18, 'For Christ died for sins once for all, the righteous for the unrighteous, to bring you to God.'

MOURNING OTHER PEOPLE'S MISFORTUNE

If we love the people around us, it's inevitable that we'll hurt when they hurt and that we will mourn the misfortune of others. There are excellent precedents for this in the Bible. Luke records that Jesus wept over His own people, Israel, less than a week before

His crucifixion. Apparently, as He caught sight of Jerusalem, which was the heart of the Jewish nation and the focus of the whole religion (thanks to the temple), His heart was wrenched with emotion. We read:

> As he approached Jerusalem and saw the city, he wept over it and said, 'If you, even you, had only known on this day what would bring you peace – but now it is hidden from your eyes. The days will come upon you when your enemies will build an embankment against you and encircle you and hem you in on every side. They will dash you to the ground, you and the children within your walls. They will not leave one stone on another, because you did not recognise the time of God's coming to you.' (Luke 19:41–44)

Jesus was following in the tradition of the prophets in feeling this kind of emotion over His own nation. In the Psalms one writer says, 'Streams of tears flow from my eyes, for your law is not obeyed' (Psalm 119:136). The prophet Jeremiah expressed similar sentiments: 'Oh, that my head were a spring of water and my eyes a fountain of tears! I would weep day and night for the slain of my people' (Jeremiah 9:1).

This may present us with a challenge if we're in the habit of giving thanks to God, saying: 'Thank you, Lord, for everything in my life' – while we forget to pray for and care about other people. Some of us may even find ourselves inadvertently judging other people, saying, 'Well, they probably deserve it,' or 'They need to learn to do something for themselves, instead of expecting other people to help them all the time.' In our individualistic culture we look after ourselves and we see our responsibility as going no further than ourselves or just, perhaps, our family. This beatitude makes it clear that we're very wrong if we have this attitude – we're supposed to be mourning for other people too.

Before you shrug your shoulders and conclude that none of this applies to you, let me challenge you a bit further. Are you sure you're not ever guilty of any form of gloating? As well as 'minding your own business' do you ever *enjoy* the suffering of other people? Isn't a great deal of television and film humour, from Chaplin to Mr Bean and beyond, based on people delighting in disasters which people inflict on themselves? The Germans even have a word for this: *Schadenfreude*, which means taking pleasure from someone else's misfortune. (Apparently *Schadenfreude* was the only form of humour that Hitler appreciated, which may help explain his deviant heart.) Of course, *Schadenfreude* is a million miles away from sympathy and light years away from Christian love. There is a particularly unpleasant (but oh so tempting) form of this that some religious or moral people suffer from – a sort of holy *Schadenfreude* where they believe that misfortune is deserved. I'm sure you know the sort of thing: the gloating that takes place when an incurable IT meddler loses all his own data; the delight when the snobbish fashion fiend spills food on her new outfit; the feeling of private satisfaction when the office bully gets bullied herself. We've all heard the comments (and some of us have made them): 'Serves him right!', 'Couldn't have happened to a more appropriate person!' or 'Nice to see a bit of justice!'

This is one of the many areas in life where it's difficult to get the balance right. Of course, we need to uphold justice. So if, on the motorway, you're overtaken by a man who is dangerously speeding, I don't see any real moral problem in you giving a cheer when, five miles later, you see that the police have pulled him over. We're right to be delighted when good triumphs over evil, it's just that we mustn't gloat! After all, where would any of us be if the universe started operating in a perfectly just manner? 'There but for the grace of God go I' is a more appropriate response because, if we're honest, we have to admit that we're all guilty of all kinds of wrong things – such as speeding, for example, and sometimes it's just that the unlucky ones get caught. What Jesus teaches us here is that mourning is better than any form of self-righteousness. Even if someone has been thoroughly unpleasant to you, you need to feel sorry when something bad happens to them, whatever it is and however 'just' it seems. Jesus said: 'Woe to you who laugh now, for you will mourn and weep' (Luke 6:25). A few verses later the same sentiment is recorded (as well as elsewhere in the Gospels) that we are to *love* our enemies and that we are to 'Do to others as you would have them do to you' (Luke 6:31). In other words, we should mourn over *all* sin and suffering; especially that committed by 'our enemies'.

Of course, the ideas I mentioned in the context of mourning for ourselves apply here too. Mourning for others needs to be both purposefully focused and confident. We need to find out exactly what's wrong and then we need to remember and remind other people that God – and good – always wins in the end.

MOURNING THE EXTERNAL WORLD

As we've already commented, the world is in a mess. From the comfort of our homes we can see all kinds of disasters being played out on our TV screens – there are famines, fires, floods, earthquakes, wars, poverty and drought. Again, in the light of this beatitude we need to consider our reaction. Should we weep or change channels? How should we feel about the state of the world economy? What should our attitude be to the extinction of species, the destruction of rain forests, the decimation of fishing stocks, the pollution of land, sea and air? How do we respond to the news of thousands of children dying of preventable hunger on a daily basis world-wide? Should we just shake our heads in dismay or should we mourn and take action? And how should we feel about our own country? What should our attitude be towards lives that are ruined by alcohol or drugs? How should we feel about the 200,000 abortions that take place each year in the UK alone? What should we think about areas where no one dares to go out in the dark? How should we feel about the fact that almost half of all marriages fail? What should we think, feel and *do* about the increasing numbers of homeless people? Should we ignore all the people we pass who are lonely? Should we shrug our shoulders, look away, and think of something else – or should we mourn alongside other people and actively do something to help them?

I probably don't need to remind you that mourning for the world needs to be as purposeful and confident as the mourning that takes place in the other two areas we've considered. But how can we do something practical to improve things? God wants us each to play our part. We are Christ's ambassadors called to transform our world. Each one of us matters. When Mother Teresa was asked if she ever became depressed seeing that her work was a small drop in the ocean she responded by saying, 'No, we must remember that the ocean is made of millions of tiny drops.'

THE BLESSING OF BEING COMFORTED

As we've seen, this beatitude covers a vast area. It extends from natural mourning over the mess caused by life's mishaps, to the spiritual mourning over our self-inflicted rebellion against God as individuals and as a species. But the blessing is simple: God promises that all who mourn will be comforted. But what does that mean?

There are problems with the word *comforter* in English. It has a rather sentimental, cosy, soothing sound to it, as in: 'When she was ill, she was comforted by the presence of her cat.' Matters are not helped when we consult the dictionary. We find that a 'comforter' refers to a) a quilted bedcover, b) a narrow, long, typically woollen neck scarf and c) a baby's dummy. In fact, the word has changed its meaning in English over the years. Originally, 'to comfort' meant 'to bring strength', since it was derived from the Latin *con fortis*, which means 'with strength'. This idea of 'reinforcing' 'or 'upholding' reflects the Greek much better than the modern English word 'comfort'. In other words, Jesus is talking about not just soothing, but strengthening those who suffer. A related Greek word is used of the Holy Spirit, who is acting, in some sense, as Jesus' successor on earth: He still helps and comforts His followers today.

In this beatitude, the source of comfort is Jesus Himself. In case your initial reaction is to think, 'Ah! You're reading something into the text that isn't there!', let's spend a moment considering the background to Jesus' words here.

The people who heard Jesus speaking would have known the word 'comfort' because they would have been very familiar with their Scriptures – in particular, the book of Isaiah, which was held in special regard. While the first thirty-nine chapters of the book of Isaiah centre on God's judgement over sin, the later chapters – from Isaiah 40 onwards – look forward to the future with great hope. It is here that we find the prediction that God will rescue His people by means of a Messiah, a 'Servant', who through suffering will save God's people (Isaiah 42:1–7; 49:1–6; 50:4–9; 52:13 – 53:12). The people listening to Jesus preaching what has come to be known as the Sermon on the Mount would have understood that Jesus was clearly making a direct reference to these verses. The idea that a Messiah would come and rescue them was crucial at the time because these people were living in oppression under Roman rule.

Now the pivotal moment of Isaiah, the point at which daylight breaks into the gloom, are the very first words of Isaiah 40:

Comfort, comfort my people, says your God. Speak tenderly to Jerusalem, and proclaim to her that her hard service has been completed, that her sin has been paid for, that she has received from the LORD's hand double for all her sins. A voice of one calling: 'In the desert prepare the way for the LORD; make straight in the wilderness a highway for our God. Every valley shall be raised up, every mountain and hill made low; the rough ground shall become level, the rugged places a plain. And the glory of the LORD will be revealed, and all mankind together will see it. For the mouth of the LORD has spoken.' (Isaiah 40:1–5)

According to Matthew and Luke, John the Baptist quoted the last part of these verses when he announced that the promised deliverer, the Messiah, had finally come (Matthew 3:1–3; Luke 3:1–6). Furthermore, according to Luke, Jesus deliberately applied other verses from Isaiah to Himself. In Luke 4:16–19 we read:

He went to Nazareth, where he had been brought up, and on the Sabbath day he went into the synagogue, as was his custom. And he stood up to read. The scroll of the prophet Isaiah was handed to him. Unrolling it, he found the place where it is written: 'The Spirit of the Lord is on me, because he has anointed me to preach good news to the poor. He has sent me to proclaim freedom for the prisoners and recovery of sight for the blind, to release the oppressed, to proclaim the year of the Lord's favour.'

It seems plain from this, and other passages, that Jesus saw Himself as the servant, the one who brings comfort and encouragement in different ways to the imprisoned, the ill and the oppressed. Other people clearly recognised Him in this way too. Jesus' followers were in no doubt that He was the one who brought comfort to all who struggled with life and sin. The church has affirmed this same belief ever since.

So when Jesus spoke of mourners 'being comforted', His

audience would have thought of this verse in Isaiah with its message of consolation and the verses that followed which speak of the great servant, the promised Messiah. To them it would not have been like the words of a politician at some disaster, who might then walk away without doing anything. Like no one else before or since, Jesus offered a way forward though the wasteland of grief and despair by His actions afterwards – dying on the cross and paying the price for our sinfulness. If the Bible teaches that grief is to be faced and expressed, it also teaches that it is bearable because there is an answer. The God who is our heavenly Father does care for us. Jesus promised His disciples at the Last Supper, 'your grief will turn to joy', and 'No one will take away your joy' (John 16:20, 22). Peter speaks of believers rejoicing in hope even though they have to suffer grief in all kinds of trials 'for a little while' (1 Peter 1:6, NLT). In heaven, grief is wiped out; joy is the emotion of eternity (Revelation 21:4). The mourners will indeed be comforted! For a person who has trusted in Christ, even the deepest and darkest night will end and grief will be replaced by joy.

There is a deep spiritual logic to all this because when someone becomes a Christian, they become deeply linked to Jesus Christ. (Two common ideas in the New Testament are either Christ being 'in us' or us being 'in Christ'; paradoxically they mean the same thing.) There are at least two implications that follow from this.

The first implication is that as Christ has already died and risen, he cannot die again and so for those who are joined with him, the worst elements of death are already neutralised. Jesus claimed, 'I am the resurrection and the life. He who believes in me will live, even though he dies; and whoever lives and believes in me will never die' (John 11:25–26). In the book of Revelation, Jesus also says, 'I am the First and the Last. I am the Living One; I was dead, and behold I am alive for ever and ever! And I hold the keys of death and Hades' (Revelation 1:17–18). Paul expresses the logic like this: 'For since death came through a man, the resurrection of the dead comes also through a man. For as in Adam all die, so in Christ all will be made alive. But each in his own turn: Christ, the first fruits; then, when he comes, those who belong to him' (1 Corinthians 15:21–23).

The second implication rests upon the Bible's claim that the dreadful power of death lies in its association with sin. God cannot 'just forgive us' because that would involve him in injustice. In a moral universe sin must be punished. The Bible reveals that God resolves the dilemma of His love being in conflict with His justice in the most daring and costly way: He came personally in Christ to suffer on the cross and pay the penalty for our wrongdoing Himself, through that sacrifice. The fact that God demands justice means that a penalty cannot be imposed twice. (Not even the Inland Revenue requires us to pay a bill twice!) So the price of sin has been paid, and for those who are in Christ that means the worst elements of death are defused. In 1 Corinthians 15:55–57 Paul writes: 'Where, O death, is your victory? Where, O death, is your sting? The sting of death is sin, and the power of sin is the law. But thanks be to God! He gives us the victory through our Lord Jesus Christ.'

So in this beatitude, Jesus speaks to people who have accepted His sacrifice and committed themselves to Him. In the book of Revelation there are troubling visions of the future but also passages of awesome comfort. The destiny of God's people is described as the following: '. . . Never again will they hunger; never again will they thirst. The sun will not beat upon them, nor any scorching heat. For the Lamb at the centre of the throne will be their shepherd; he will lead them to springs of living water. And God will wipe away every tear from their eyes' (Revelation 7:16–17). At the very end of the book we read:

Then I saw a new heaven and a new earth, for the first heaven and the first earth had passed away, and there was no longer any sea. I saw the Holy City, the new Jerusalem, coming down out of heaven from God, prepared as a bride beautifully dressed for her husband. And I heard a loud voice from the throne saying, 'Now the dwelling of God is with men, and he will live with them. They will be his people, and God himself will be with them and be their God. He will wipe every tear from their eyes. There will be no more death or mourning or crying or pain, for the old order of things has passed away.' (Revelation 21:1–4)

You will have noticed that I have used more biblical passages here than I do elsewhere. The reason is simple: the finest words, the best logic and the most elegant philosophy cannot ultimately even begin to ease the horrors of suffering and death. The only enduring antidote to mourning over what life can do to us lies in the hope God offers us in Christ.

THE BLESSING OF COMFORTING

It is not Christian to be uncaring and emotionless because God embodies love, not indifference. He is love itself. Being indifferent to suffering means denying everything that makes us human: love, emotion, reason, care and compassion. Seen in this light, although grief is still unpleasant, feeling it at least demonstrates that we're human. If we can no longer weep, we might ask whether we are, in any real sense, still alive. A stoical outlook must be resisted because it offers no comfort to anyone; it doesn't demonstrate our love for God and it denies us the blessing of comforting others.

The Bible suggests emotionally healthy ways to mourn. It doesn't encourage us to suppress or be ashamed of our sorrow – it's far too realistic for that. Almost every major figure in the Bible mourns something at some point: Abraham (Genesis 23:2), Jacob (Genesis 37:24), David (2 Samuel 12:15; 2 Samuel 18:33), Jeremiah (Jeremiah 9:1), Job (Job 1:20) and Paul (Acts 20:31). Even Jesus himself mourned. As Isaiah had prophesied, the servant of the Lord was 'a man of sorrows, and familiar with suffering' (Isaiah 53:3). As well as weeping at the state of Jerusalem, He wept at the grave of His friend Lazarus (John 11:35) and He also 'offered up prayers and petitions with loud cries and tears' at other times (Hebrews 5:7). Members of the early church also did a lot of weeping – despite their belief in the resurrection. We read that 'Godly men buried Stephen and mourned deeply for him' (Acts 8:2); Paul reports that he 'served the Lord with great humility and with tears' (Acts 20:19). When he said goodbye to the Ephesian elders, 'They all wept as they embraced him and kissed him' (Acts 20:37). We also learn that there were degrees of their grief because the next verse says, 'What grieved them most was his statement that they would never see his face again' (Acts 20:37–38). The book of Ecclesiastes says that there's 'a time to weep and a time to laugh, a time to mourn and a time to dance' (Ecclesiastes 3:4). Clearly, the Bible portrays mourning and sorrow as a necessary part of life.

Given these precedents involving key biblical figures, including Jesus himself, it would be absurd to try and escape our grief or to expect it to disappear as our Christian faith develops. Instead, we should see it as an inevitable part of human experience, which can prompt us to compassionate action.

How can we best comfort other people, though? We need to recognise that people respond differently to grief and some take longer than others to recover. We need to recognise that people are not immature or weak if they need more time to work through the grieving process – cheery comments might actually make matters worse. Rationalising suffering might be just as bad, and mourning should certainly never prompt us to defend God. A friend told me how his boss at work suddenly confronted him. She blurted out that a colleague's young daughter had just died and then, amid tears, demanded, 'And where's your God in that?' As my friend fortunately realised, the very last thing that she (or the family) required at that moment was a theological justification. What *was* needed was sympathy, shared grief and prayer for comfort.

Above all, when we share in other people's mourning and comfort them, we should be confident of God's justice, and His promise to all who accept His word and ask Jesus into their lives.

TO SUM UP

Perhaps no beatitude appears at first glance to offer so little, but on examination to give so much. The first beatitude announced that the poor in spirit – those who recognised their need of God – were blessed. This second announces the blessedness of those who grieve and mourn over that very same poor spiritual state. This idea of being so sorry that we lament or grieve over what we are probably strikes us as very strange. Today, the mood is to boast about ourselves, even if we have nothing in which to boast. The rich often go so far as to have a publicist to manage their image – and the rest of us might wish we could afford that particular luxury. In our society, no one usually admits guilt – think of the implications for the 'no claims bonus'! – and certainly no one grieves over their sins. Even in the case of some major breach of trust or morality, the best we may get is a formal admission of 'inappropriate behaviour' (generally read by a solicitor) and a sheepish grin before the cameras. In many cases, the nearest anyone comes to a confession is a lucrative, double-page 'tell all' spread in a tabloid.

Once again this beatitude flies in the face of all that our culture stands for. We have elevated pleasure to such a degree that we shun not just mourning, but also any sort of seriousness. The pressure is on us to be party people, bouncing from one supposedly joyful event to another. Well, perhaps it's time to get serious about seriousness. Now please don't get me wrong here. I do believe in enjoyment, laughter and humour. (Why else do you think I've called this book *The Happiness Secret*?) I'm just saying that the refusal of our society to face up to serious issues is almost pathological and, as Jesus has shown us, *unhelpful* in terms of making ourselves happy. We have become so scared of seriousness that we avoid very important matters. For instance, as a minister I often have personal conversations with people where I challenge them about that most serious of all subjects, the need to get right with God. Often, when they see that they are at a crossroads and are faced with a choice, they will suddenly try and make a joke as if hoping to create a smokescreen of laughter, which will allow them the opportunity to escape. In many areas of life, we have come to prize the flippant joke, the amusing one-liner, the quick put-down, instead of any serious, carefully considered response.

Yet here, as elsewhere in our culture, there is an extraordinary inconsistency. Deep down, we do (perhaps reluctantly) recognise the value of solemnity and seriousness. For a start, we want our leaders to be serious people. Any politician who, at a time of great crisis, misjudges the public mood and cracks some light-hearted quip is asking for trouble. It is interesting, for example, that although Winston Churchill is remembered as a great speaker, it is not his often wickedly amusing comments that are most quoted, but those solemn phrases from speeches given in times of despair.

With this beatitude and its emphasis on mourning we have reached the lowest point in the Beatitudes. From now on the road runs uphill. We now discover how Jesus builds on this foundation of weakness to reassure His people of a better future.

3

Be Meek

Blessed are the meek,
for they will inherit the earth.
(Matthew 5:5)

MODERN-DAY 'MEEKNESS'

I would imagine that when you look at this beatitude, you might wonder who on earth would want to be meek. It's not exactly an appealing state of existence. We might not mind being called 'poor in spirit' or being known as someone who 'mourns'. But meek? Hardly. It calls up the most unhappy images: mild-mannered Clark Kent bumbling his way around the office of the *Daily Planet*, the co-worker who is always ignored at staff meetings; the man persuaded by the car salesman that yes, he really does want the purple model that's been sitting on the forecourt for months; the woman who always mumbles, 'Whatever you say, dear' to her husband, no matter what he says. Almost no concept goes against the spirit of the age more than meekness. To believe in meekness seems to be to join the ranks of life's losers. As the saying goes: 'The meek shall inherit the earth ... if that's OK with everyone else.'

Apart from being unfashionable and unpalatable, being meek really doesn't seem to make any practical sense. The word 'meek' doesn't just rhyme with 'weak', it's pretty much identical. In today's world, to be meek is to be powerless and that is one thing we don't want to be. Who wants to be meek when you have to pull out into a manic stream of rush-hour traffic? Who wants to be meek when attempting to return some defective item to a sales manager who really isn't bothered? Who wants to be meek when you're negotiating over a house and any flinching may mean you can't afford it at all? Yet Jesus says the meek will inherit the earth! How can this be?

Nowadays it's seen as particularly ineffectual for men to be meek – but a double standard is in operation. If you listen carefully you quite often hear statements that seem to go like this: 'He's a go-getter, but she's aggressive', 'He's a high achiever, but she's just pushy', 'He's assertive, but she's bossy'. It's almost as if we still hold on to the ancient rule that a man should never be meek while a woman should never be anything else. In fact, I think men and women have differing but equally challenging temptations in this area of power and meekness. While violence is generally considered a bad thing in both men and women, men are at least expected to *look* tough and both men and women are expected to talk tough. The rule of our times seems to be that we mustn't *show* any weakness.

Actually, not only is meekness scorned everywhere, but its counterparts – confidence and assertiveness – are widely praised. We read an article in a magazine celebrating a woman who has gone from being penniless to abundantly rich, largely thanks to her determined and ruthless business practices. A friend tells us about a man who has now negotiated vastly improved working conditions using belligerent tactics with his boss. We hear a colleague admiringly explaining how a mutual acquaintance got her plane seat upgraded to Business Class by throwing her weight around at the airport check-in. Almost everywhere we look, life's prizes are taken by the assertive, the determined and the pushy.

Meekness is such a negative feature that many of us have friends, colleagues or even spouses whom we wish were a little bit less meek because we spend a lot of our time rescuing them from the difficulties that this very characteristic has caused. We've all heard, or even uttered, exasperated comments like these: 'What do you mean, you promised to work nights?', 'You actually agreed to buy it like that?' or 'Why didn't you demand your money back?' Of all the upside-down notions that the Christian faith offers, this one appears to be the most nonsensical.

MEEKNESS IN THE ROMAN EMPIRE

Before you reject the idea of being meek let me ask you a question. Do you really think this beatitude was any easier to follow when it was first given? In fact, the world Jesus lived in was even tougher on the meek than it is today. It was a time and place where bullying was very much a way of life. Passing Roman soldiers could simply seize on any man and get him to carry their packs. (But only for one mile! They could be punished if they demanded more. Hence the phrase 'going the second mile', which disempowers the bully.) The priests and the rich were not much below them in the brutality stakes. The concept of 'human rights' didn't even exist. There was no institutional protection of the weak through pensions, a health service or legal aid. In those days when someone said, 'They'll crucify me for this,' they weren't using a figure of speech. In Jesus' day, you could all too easily end up being crucified, stoned or condemned to permanent slavery. In other words, when Jesus said that the meek were going to be blessed, He would have been very definitely greeted by the first-century equivalent of 'Pull the other leg!'

Jesus was speaking at a turbulent time in the history of the Jewish people. The Romans were in charge and they showed no inclination to surrender power. As a result there was a lively debate among the Jews as to whether or not an armed rebellion ought to be attempted. There was a growing movement of revolution-aries (generally categorised as 'the Zealots') and they no doubt used expressions such as 'bringing about the kingdom of God by force'.

The idea that this is the context of this beatitude is hinted at in the blessing, which, in modern English, we translate as 'they will inherit the earth'. We will refer to this phrase later, but here you ought to realise that the word used for 'earth' could also mean 'land'. In fact, Jesus is probably making a reference here either to Psalm 25:13 or Psalm 37:11, where the Psalmist talks about people inheriting 'the land'. In the Psalms this almost certainly applies only to 'the Promised Land' – that small patch of territory between the River Jordan and the Mediterranean Sea. In fact, the Old Testament term is also ambiguous, which is why by Jesus' time some Jewish people were expecting God's people to reign over all the earth. Nevertheless, the Jewish nationalists of Jesus' day would no doubt have understood his reference to 'the land/earth' as specifically applying to their very own Promised Land. On this basis, what Jesus says is very striking: it will be the meek, not the armed or the powerful, who will inherit the land. In other words, Jesus was taking a stand against any uprising or rebellion. Interestingly enough, a generation later, faced with a Roman occu-pation of incompetence, brutality and greed, a violent revolt did begin and the appalling result was that in AD 70 the Jewish nation was brutally crushed by the Romans. Jerusalem was almost levelled to the ground; the temple was utterly obliterated and the Jewish faith and people very nearly joined it.

Now it is a fairly reasonable guess that the majority of the readers of this book are not terribly interested in armed political revolution. We are, however, all deeply concerned about our own dignity and value. We resent being put down or treated as infe-riors by anyone, whether it is members of our family, our bosses, the local council, the government or the bureaucrats of the European

Community. I'm sure, at some stage, you have been fairly close to someone who has walked out of a job. I have heard remarks like this: 'I've had enough. I told them that if that was all the worth they placed on my work then there was no point in me staying.' Or, 'I told them that I no longer felt valued, that I had had enough of being trampled on, and that I wanted to go somewhere where I was taken seriously.' This beatitude therefore addresses these all-too-relevant questions of our own worth and value, and how we see ourselves.

The ancient Greeks also strongly disliked not just the word 'meek' but the whole idea of 'meekness'. Theirs was a society based on slavery; so to aspire to meekness was to suggest that you wanted to be a slave (a state very definitely to be avoided). These views have persisted. In the nineteenth century, the German philosopher Friedrich Nietzsche, who was obsessed with the idea of human development centring on power, saw this praising of weakness as embodying 'the slave morality of Christianity'. He viewed Christianity as a conspiracy of the powerful to keep weak people down.

So, having set out the considerable difficulties for understanding meekness in both ancient and modern times, let's now unpack what this beatitude means. I think you will find yourself intrigued by the outcome, mainly because we get some pleasant surprises if we differentiate between meekness as it's commonly understood and *true* meekness as Jesus defined it.

FALSE MEEKNESS

I suspect there are many types of false meekness. Let's consider just four of them.

One type of false meekness (almost certainly the lowest form) is the deliberate pretence at meekness. It is most spectacularly seen when some celebrity turns up and does some kind of community work – laying a brick wall, or perhaps planting a tree. The trouble here is that they've arranged it as a photo opportunity. Not a hair is out of place and the casual clothes are planned. This is not meekness, it's merely poorly disguised pride. How can humility be real when a person is proud of it? It can also be used as a manipulative ploy, as in Charles Dickens' Mr Micawber.

A second type of false meekness originates from low self-esteem. This occurs when someone decides they have to give in, because that's what they always do. You can almost hear them saying to themselves, 'I'm hopeless, a born loser. I might as well get on with being last as that's what I always do.' Incidentally, I suspect it's this attitude that gets people most worried about meekness. There are a lot of people with low self-esteem out there and anything that seems to encourage this rather pathetic state is not a good idea. True meekness is very different, however, and in the case of someone with healthy self-esteem, it suggests the person has nothing to prove. The Christian view is that all human beings have enormous value by virtue of being made in the image of God and this in itself is an antidote to low self-esteem.

Another type of false meekness is making excuses for failure. When talented people underachieve, it's unlikely to be as a result of meekness. True meekness should never smother ambition or prevent someone aspiring for excellence. Meekness should never be an excuse for mediocrity. Of course, whenever a person wins a prize for sport, music or writing he or she should be humble before God and gracious towards others, but meekness should never prevent a person from achieving.

The fourth type of false meekness I'd like to mention is perhaps the saddest type of all. It arises out of a need to be liked. Imagine someone does something wrong at work, but a colleague fails to say anything about it. This wouldn't be a case of genuine meekness but would probably be a sign that the colleague didn't want to cause offence or make an enemy. His desire to be liked would have prevented him from doing the right thing, which is not meekness. The irony, though, is that people aren't fools and they soon notice when we don't challenge them. Instead of considering a silent colleague to be a friend, most people are more likely to decide that they are spineless, so any previous friendship is likely to become devalued. Wise people value friends who tell them when they're doing something wrong.

In all probability, when people feel they can't accept 'meekness', they are rejecting one of these pathetic types of false meekness, not the kind of meekness that Jesus had in mind.

TRUE MEEKNESS

The meaning of the Greek

The Greek word that is generally translated as 'meek' in the Sermon on the Mount occurs in three other places in the New Testament (Matthew 11:29; 21:5; 1 Peter 3:4) and it is generally translated as 'gentle'. Outside the New Testament, the Greek word is used in the context of tamed animals, soothing medicine or a soft breeze on a hot day. You are probably getting the picture. We could say that to 'be meek' is to be gentle, humble, considerate, courteous, docile, amiable and teachable. You could even argue that it extends as far as being kind or even friendly.

THE ANTITHESIS OF MEEKNESS

One way of understanding meekness as Jesus defined it is to consider its opposite. This is a particularly helpful approach because we can then see meekness as the opposite of what might be considered a complete A to Z of negative personality traits. Let me list just a few adjectives that are the opposite of meek: aggressive, arrogant, assertive, big-headed, bitter, bullying, caustic, domineering, egotistical, greedy, macho, malicious, obstinate, oppressive, pretentious, proud, pushy, ruthless, selfish, self-centred, severe, tyrannical, unteachable, vengeful, wrathful. (I couldn't come up with a word for every letter of the alphabet, but Z could perhaps be 'zeal for your own glory'!) You get the point. At first hearing no one may care for 'meekness' or 'gentleness' but no one likes its alternatives. In fact, just look at that list. How many of the things are included that make life unpleasant? If you had to characterise the people who give you problems, wouldn't you use just those words to describe them? Also, have you noticed how few of the attitudes listed above are associated with happiness? Consider the following pairs of adjectives: 'aggrieved and happy', 'greedy and contented', 'vengeful and peaceful'. I think you'll agree that they don't sit well together. It is worth understanding that Jesus is not only elevating meekness as a virtue in its own right, but also depicting a virtue which stands in direct opposition to a wide range of unpleasant and undesirable mental states.

HUMILITY BEFORE GOD

You will remember that the first two beatitudes focused on what we might call 'fundamental attitudes', which affect our relationship to God. However, this beatitude is concerned not only with our relationship towards God, but also with our relationships with others. Here Jesus asks His followers to show humility before God and gentleness towards others.

Being humble before God means admitting that we're corrupt and frail, with limited and flawed knowledge of all things. At the same time, it means admitting that God is perfect and eternal and that He has a total knowledge of how things are. On that basis, being meek means saying: 'God, you know best.' This is far from easy because the Bible makes it clear that at the root of our natural instinct is an ancient and deep-seated inclination to rebel against God. It is at the heart of the story of Adam and Eve recounted in the first three chapters of the Bible. In the blissful life of total harmony, rather than being meek and dependent on God, these first people choose to be independent and assert their freedom, believing that they know best. Their descendants, you and I, have a built-in tendency to operate in the same manner.

Another aspect of meekness before God is acknowledging our own weakness. When we come to God in this meek spirit, we then receive His strength. St Paul knew this secret to happiness very well. Before he encountered Jesus Christ, Paul was known throughout the ancient world as a strong, bold and arrogant leader against Christians. He was on a personal campaign to kill Christians. He was boastful in his approach. After Paul meets Jesus on the road to Damascus, we see a total transformation in his character. This once macho character speaks about his weakness in this way: 'So now I am glad to boast about my weaknesses, so that the power of Christ can work through me. That's why I take pleasure in my weaknesses, and in the insults, hardships, persecutions, and troubles that I suffer for Christ. For when I am weak, then I am strong' (2 Corinthians 12:9–10, NLT). Paul reveals to us one of the most extraordinary mysteries of being a Christian – when we come before God in meekness, we are then filled with the supernatural strength of God. This strength is far beyond what any human could muster up alone. This is why Paul says, 'I know what it is to be in need, and I know what it is to have plenty. I have learned the secret of being content in any and every situation, whether well fed or hungry, whether living in plenty or in want. I can do everything through him who gives me strength' (Philippians 4:12–13). God longs for our meek spirit so that He can fill us with His mighty Spirit.

GENTLENESS TOWARDS PEOPLE

Gentleness towards other people means being kind to them, taking pains to put up with them, encouraging them, and not belittling them in any way. It means holding back from saying that a colleague is a fool when in fact they are behaving foolishly. It means acting in a quiet way when someone blows it. It means standing alongside someone in support and not towering above them in judgement. Paul expresses the essence of a meek spirit in his letter to the Corinthians. In this letter he describes meekness and love in action. He writes, 'Love is patient and kind. Love is not jealous or boastful or proud or rude. It does not demand its own way. It is not irritable, and it keeps no record of being wronged. It does not rejoice about injustice but rejoices whenever the truth wins out' (1 Corinthians 13:4–6, NLT). A meek person approaches others with this kind of love.

JESUS AS AN EXAMPLE OF MEEKNESS

As with the other beatitudes, in the case of meekness Jesus gave us a perfect model throughout His life on earth. Given this, it's not surprising that His teaching carried such authority. At the end of the Sermon on the Mount we read: 'When Jesus had finished saying these things, the crowds were amazed at his teaching, because he taught as one who had authority, and not as their teachers of the law' (Matthew 7:28–29). Part of this perceived authority was what we might call 'authenticity' because He really did 'walk the talk'. In other words, when Jesus spoke of how we ought to live, people saw that He lived out every word He spoke. In fact, Jesus is the only teacher in human history who has lived up perfectly to the standards of His own teaching. Jesus is the only person who has lived a flawless, sinless life.

Jesus put on no airs of superiority. He walked among the weakest and the poorest of society. He had time for those people for whom the men in authority had no time: the sick, the demonised, the diseased, the downtrodden and even women and children, which would have been astonishing in His culture. He took upon Himself the title of servant (Mark 10:45; Luke 22:27) and even stooped to the task of washing people's feet, something that was usually done by servants. Yet with Jesus, the meekness was never weakness (or even 'mildness'). When we read the Gospels it is evident that an unshakeable toughness lies at Jesus' core. From dealing with the attitudes of the disciples to opposing the Pharisees, Jesus was and is a constant source of steady strength.

What is particularly worth noting is that Jesus could clearly have had far more popular support than He actually allowed if it hadn't been for His meekness. Repeatedly it's reported that He deliberately tried to defuse public enthusiasm. In some cases He left an area in order to avoid mindless political adulation, and on one occasion He made Himself scarce when people wanted to make Him king (John 6:15). These are all indications that Jesus made true meekness a fundamental principle of His life.

In Philippians 2:5–11, we learn that Jesus' meekness is part of the wider biblical narrative. Paul, writing to a divided church at Philippi, says, almost as an aside, that they really ought to have the attitude of Jesus and he explains how this attitude fitted into the bigger picture:

> Your attitude should be the same as that of Christ Jesus: Who, being in very nature God, did not consider equality with God something to be grasped, but made himself nothing, taking the very nature of a servant, being made in human likeness. And being found in appearance as a man, he humbled himself and

became obedient to death – even death on a cross! Therefore God exalted him to the highest place and gave him the name that is above every name, that at the name of Jesus every knee should bow, in heaven and on earth and under the earth, and every tongue confess that Jesus Christ is Lord, to the glory of God the Father. (Philippians 2:5–11)

This passage is often used to explain how Jesus really was both God and truly human. What is significant for us now is how Jesus is portrayed as truly meek and humble. The passage explains how Christ willingly gave up what was the very ultimate in power and status (being God) to become a mere earthly human. Jesus gave the ultimate demonstration of the principle of true meekness, which means deliberately yielding personal power and status in order to serve others. Our modern-day equivalent might be the CEO standing in line for coffee, the ship's captain cleaning the decks, the minister cleaning the kitchen, the chief administrator giving the caretaker a helping hand. In other words, true meekness always involves some sort of descent from higher status. Jesus said that he 'did not come to be served, but to serve, and to give his life as a ransom for many' (Mark 10:45).

YIELDING POWER APPROPRIATELY

As we can see from Jesus' example, meekness involves the considered and deliberate yielding of personal power. In other words, our personal power is not taken away from us when we become Christians, but given up voluntarily, with prayerful thought.

It is important to remember that meekness does not mean silence or inaction. Meekness can never involve agreeing with your line manager's dilution of quality so the customer gets an inferior product. This would be moral weakness, not true meekness. You could argue, as some have, that Hitler was only ever able rise to power because the German church suffered an excess of the wrong sort of meekness.

When considering how meekness relates to *giving up* power we must also note that it is only possible when the power is ours to 'give up'. It would be irresponsible for a teacher, a policeman or a prison warden to give up power and allow rules to be bent, or for a bank manager to give away money belonging to the bank. No one has the right to yield authority that they hold by virtue of a position or job. Meekness is about how we manage the power we have ourselves, in our own right. Any yielding of power needs to be carefully and prayerfully thought through. Generally speaking, it is important to have well-marked and well-defended moral boundaries and to defend them whenever necessary, especially when injustice is about to be committed. Yet, as St Peter said, it is always vital to speak with gentleness and respect (1 Peter 3:15).

COMMON DIFFICULTIES WITH MEEKNESS

Clearly, it's not easy to be truly meek. It is easier to slide into false meekness or give up. I suspect the people who find true meekness fairly easy are people who were brought up in stable, affirming families, where they knew they could be open about their failings and weaknesses without being crushed. People who come from a dysfunctional family may have an altogether different experience, especially if they have repeatedly been told they're useless or that they'll achieve nothing. In the case of a person who *does* succeed despite this negative talk, meekness might be extremely difficult because it would seem like agreeing with their parents' verdict, which they had striven so hard to overcome. The wounded person is often hesitant to relinquish any sort of power for fear of being abused or overtaken. This person must not fear to be meek because

God's protection and strength far surpasses any human effort. Natural leaders might also find it particularly difficult to be meek and gentle, as might anyone emerging with psychological scars from situations where they have experienced oppression.

Even a person with few past hurts to work through might have a problem with meekness because it might make them feel vulnerable. We all have some sort of status in life, whether at home or work, and we acquire armour and defences that we use on a daily basis to protect us. We take pride in our job titles, the size of our office, who speaks to us, and in what tone they address us. One sad, but convincing, analysis of consumerism suggests that many people buy expensive 'label' goods because they feel that such brands give them status. For them, it is true that 'you are what you wear'. Meekness challenges every aspect of this because to be meek means that we put aside all such armour and defence. Doing this is threatening because it puts at risk not just our status but also our reputation, our achievements and even our wealth. Yet if we are linked to Christ, we can take this risk because we are no longer concerned about rank and status. We have a secure position as one of God's children within His family. Who we are is no longer defined by our worldly wealth, our salary or the type of car we drive, but is defined simply by the awesome and extraordinary fact that we are linked eternally to Christ.

THE BLESSINGS FOR THOSE WHO ARE TRULY MEEK

As we've already noted, Jesus promised the meek would 'inherit the earth.' This is His promise of a future inheritance for his followers. As suggested earlier, some of Jesus' original audience would probably have thought this blessing was about the physical land of Israel. Yet even while Jesus was still with the disciples on earth, people were beginning to realise that the idea of a

'Promised Land' was being superseded. Certainly when you read through the book of Acts, which records a selective history of the events of the first few decades of the church, you see how very soon after the resurrection any idea of a future centred on the physical land of Israel rapidly disappeared.

It's interesting to consider why the ancient Jews longed for the Promised Land so much. It represented two things for them: either 'prosperity and protection' or 'supply and security'. Having their own land, God's people would have the food and water they needed, and they would also be secure from enemy attack. It makes sense that this should become less important after Jesus' death and resurrection because He Himself is both our 'prosperity and protection' and our 'supply and security'. He is far more than an area of land because He supplies all we need and He protects us from all that threatens us. All that the Promised Land was to the Old Testament Jews, Jesus is to His followers today.

So what does this promise of 'inheriting the earth' mean for us today? We are not called by Jesus to look for a physical Promised Land, but instead to place our hope in a heavenly inheritance. Death is no longer something to fear because every follower of Jesus will enjoy an afterlife with Him.

In concluding that this is the meaning of this blessing we can also see the continuation of a pattern. In the first two beatitudes there was a kind of 'matching' between the characteristic and the consequence: people who are poor in spirit will be given the riches of the kingdom and people who mourn will be consoled. In this beatitude we see that those who give up power and privilege in this life will be given riches beyond comprehension in the next. An aged and penniless believer in Christ dying alone in a hospital bed is richer – where it really counts – than the fittest and richest in the world. In other words, we can afford to be meek in this life, because we know it's not all that there is. Meekness involves us temporarily giving up a little in order to permanently gain an infinitely greater amount. That seems like a pretty fair deal to me. However, we must avoid a 'pie in the sky when you die' emphasis (typical of a Victorian attitude towards the poor), because this can lead us to neglect the pursuit of justice and improved living standards for all which is part of our calling as Christians.

A PRESENT-DAY PLUS

A mindset dominated by true meekness is profoundly advantageous. After all, true meekness is an antidote to the A to Z of negative personality traits we considered earlier. Wherever disputes take place – whether in a football club, the office, at home or even in church – they're bound to be a major source of unhappiness in our lives. Trace such disputes back to their source and you'll more than likely find that they're based on issues of pride, honour or status. It is all too common to hear stories of some good venture being ruined by one of the people involved simply because the person could not achieve what he or she wanted. As the flames of the squabble are being fanned into conflict, the poisonous phrase is often uttered: 'If they don't do it my way, then they're not going to do it at all.' How many squabbles have deepened and festered because one party felt that they had to 'have the last word'? How many dismal wars, financially disastrous business ventures and disputes in marriage have arisen (and dragged on) because those involved weren't meek enough to admit that they might be wrong?

There are flameproof garments which are almost impossible to set alight. To be truly meek is to have a flameproof temperament, where the sparks of quarrels may land but are never ignited.

Meekness is also a virtue in our relationships. In office environments, for example, meek people make good team players; they work well with others because they have nothing to prove. They ask for and take advice, so they are often asked for advice themselves. Truly meek people make good researchers and good decision-makers because rather than impose their own theories on data and events, they look carefully at the facts first and listen to colleagues. They're open to the world and their motto is always: 'I may be wrong.' Paradoxically, the truly meek are also not inclined to give in to others. Since they have nothing to prove and seek no power for themselves they can actually be bolder and more forthright than those who know nothing of meekness. The man or woman who stands up to the boss and says, 'I'm afraid I think you are wrong here,' may actually be very meek. They are so full of true meekness that they have an independence of mind based on the glorious freedom that they do not actually care what anybody else thinks of them! They have one Boss and His name is God. They're trustworthy because they don't value themselves above others and have no desire for power. While other people follow the Peter Principle ('Every person is promoted to the level of their incompetence,' i.e. gets promoted to a point where they can no longer perform well. Laurence J. Peter and Raymond Hull, *The Peter Principle*, Morrow & Co., 1969), a meek person will say: 'No, I am happy in the job that I am in. I am doing it well. This is as far as I want to go. To advance beyond this would be to ask for trouble.' Can you see how meekness could speed you along the road to contentment and happiness?

Meekness is even advantageous for the perfectionists and idealists among us. The truly meek are free from the pressure some people might put themselves under to achieve. The unwritten epitaph on many gravestones might be, 'Here lies a man/woman/husband/wife/manager/employee who could not bear the possibility that they might actually be less than perfect.' The truly meek, however, are released and free from all this because they can admit that they made a mistake. There is a willingness to say 'Sorry'. With the truly meek, what you see is what you get, and everyone is better off as a result.

I have no doubt, for example, that the truly meek have more enduring marriages and better relationships with their children. They have more friends and deeper friendships with them. As you take your eyes off yourself, you can truly see and experience the earth and all it has to offer. This is why the meek inherit the earth. They are open to all its possibilities because they are not self-focused. Self-focused people are dank like the Dead Sea, having no outlet of love. However, people who focus on others are like mighty rivers flowing with life-giving waters.

TO SUM UP

Although it's easy to initially dismiss meekness as an irrelevance, I hope you can now see its importance. True meekness lies close to the heart of the happy. What we have called 'the considered and deliberate yielding of personal power' is not so much an attitude as a frame of mind. It is that principle of how we live that prefers to listen before speaking, to think before acting, to consult before ruling and to look before leaping. As we've seen, in essence, being meek involves humility before God and gentleness towards others. It has nothing to do with weakness, but everything to do with knowing who you are, accepting the possibility of being wrong occasionally (or often!) and being confident in one's own identity, while remaining 'teachable'.

Ultimately, meekness is essential if you want to follow the road to blessing and happiness. After all, only the meek read road maps!

4

Be Righteous

*Blessed are those who hunger
and thirst for righteousness,
for they will be filled.*
(Matthew 5:6)

GOAL OF A LIFETIME

Let's begin with a cautionary tale. Once upon a time there were three entrepreneurs who lived in London. They were bidding for a major contract and were surprised to hear that the final interview was to be held in the city of Bristol. On the morning of the interview, the first entrepreneur was in such a hurry to get there that he mis-programmed his car's GPS and drove to Birmingham. Of course, he was disqualified for not getting to the interview. The second entrepreneur started driving, but on the outskirts of Bristol decided that she really didn't want the bother that the contract would involve, so she turned around and drove back to London. Only the third entrepreneur actually made it to Bristol and, somewhat inevitably, was awarded the contract. The first entrepreneur had enough determination but pursued the wrong goal. The second candidate pursued the right goal but didn't have enough perseverance. Only the third candidate pursued the right goal and also had enough determination for the job. The moral of the story is that it's not just what you aim for in life, it's how you aim for it. This fourth beatitude talks about both aspects of life: setting a goal and having the determination to achieve it.

As we've seen, there's a sequence to the Beatitudes. The first two talk about the foundations that must be laid in our lives: the recognition and understanding that we have fallen far from God's standards, and how we must turn to Him in all humility to receive His grace and mercy. The third beatitude spelt out the only great means to progress: remaining meek and teachable. The fourth beatitude, which we are considering in this chapter, focuses on our destination and journey in life, i.e. our goal and the determination we need to get there. Jesus indicates here that our goal needs to be righteousness and the fact that He says we need to 'hunger and thirst' for it suggests we need to be determined if we are to reach it.

This beatitude effectively introduces us to two unfamiliar concepts: the idea of righteousness and the need to long for it intensely. They are both linked with happiness inasmuch as they confirm that the worldly quest for happiness itself is misguided. As we've no doubt experienced in our own lives, hungering after worldly things such as sex, money and power will always lead to dissatisfaction. However, half-baked efforts to succeed at righteousness are also likely to be unfulfilling. While we would ideally like to hear Jesus suggesting we search for happiness, we find here that He says we should make *righteousness* our goal instead. And while we would ideally like to have things fall into our laps, this verse is a sharp reminder that more effort is required.

CONFUSION ABOUT 'RIGHTEOUSNESS'

Since our politicians need to be re-elected they do an enormous amount of market research on what the public want to hear. They calculate the public mood and focus their speeches on what appeals to society. These days, politicians highlight prosperity, health, security for ourselves, environmental protection and global justice – as long as it doesn't adversely affect us personally! And nowhere on any national agenda do you ever find the word 'righteousness'.

Since righteousness isn't one of society's goals, it is understandable that many people don't seem very sure what it means. If ever the word was understood, it's now become an obscure, time-worn museum piece, which is honoured but of uncertain significance. We might guess from the fact that it's got 'right' in it that the word 'righteousness' relates to good things. However, that seems to be as far as our comprehension of righteousness extends.

In Jesus' day, by contrast, Judea was full of people claiming to be 'righteous' and there was probably no shortage of people offering the 'right way to righteousness'. Some of the Dead Sea Scrolls from the time of Jesus discuss a figure called the 'Teacher of Righteousness'. His identity, though, like much to do with the Scrolls, remains unconfirmed. Nevertheless, this does seem to be a pointer to the fact that righteousness was very much on the agenda at the time of Jesus.

Today there is a theological debate on what righteousness actually means. It's a major debate that has raged for centuries simply because it deals with the most important issue of all: how we get right with God. The question as to how men and women might gain righteousness lies at the heart of the great disputes of the Reformation, which divided Christendom in the fifteenth and sixteenth centuries. The great cultural fault line between Protestant and Catholic Europe, which still exists today, is also a division based on this single word.

Fortunately, there is at least some degree of agreement. Both parties agree that the word 'righteousness' centres on how God views us and whether we are 'right' with Him. To be 'right' with God simply means to be in a right relationship with Him. This means exactly what it does with any other person, i.e. to have no unresolved issues, no grievances, and no unsettled debts. But beyond this there are many differences of opinion.

Some people say that righteousness is a word to describe our actions – what we *do*. Within this view, a righteous man or woman is someone who does right things, including such things as praying, fasting, giving money to the poor and standing up for justice and truth. According to this view, the actual *doing* of certain things makes a person righteous. Other people say it is irrelevant what we do and instead they see righteousness as a state or condition, like being declared not guilty by a judge or being adopted into a family. They claim it is not about what we do, but what we *are*. They say that being righteous is the result of being declared righteous by God, who bestows righteousness as a free gift, through 'grace'. Our role is to simply accept this new status by faith.

The idea that we can *work our way* to righteousness is problematic for various reasons. For a start, if God's standard is perfection, how can anyone achieve righteousness? If the pass mark is 100 per cent surely we *all* fail? Jesus' own teaching suggests that human effort is inadequate. No one worked harder at attaining righteousness than the Pharisees, but Jesus said, 'For I tell you that unless your righteousness surpasses that of the Pharisees and the teachers of the law, you will certainly not enter the kingdom of heaven' (Matthew 5:20). And, even if we could achieve this righteousness, how could we maintain it? How could anyone hope to stay righteous until they made it safely to life's finishing line? The fear of a last-minute stumble has haunted many good people. This distressing worry about achieving and maintaining a state of righteousness seems at odds with the fact that in the New Testament the followers of Jesus are joyfully confident that they are right – and *permanently* right – with God.

Another question that arises with the view that we can earn our *own* righteousness is this: why did Jesus die? The whole New

Testament echoes with the joyful news that it is Jesus' death on the cross that has made peace between God and men. If we are made righteous by our own good actions why was the cross necessary? Also, why is the message about Jesus and His death referred to as the 'good news'? What, we might ask, is either 'good' or 'news' about an 'earn-your-way-to-heaven' faith?

Even if we conclude that Jesus' death made us right with God, the constant reference to righteousness in the Bible doesn't make sense if our change in status is final. (The words 'righteous' and 'righteousness' appear 512 times throughout the Bible, 135 of them in the New Testament.) The gift of eternal righteousness (being right with God) would suggest that we no longer need to worry about *earning* our way to heaven and into a right relationship with God. However, this view could lead to people thinking they have free licence to do whatever they wanted. This in itself would wreck any idea of living good lives and would make all those New Testament letters that talk about avoiding evil nonsensical (Romans 5:15 – 6:4).

WHAT IT MEANS TO BE RIGHTEOUS

There is no doubt that the basis for our righteousness is God's gift of forgiveness. The Bible makes it clear that we are made right with God by faith in Jesus Christ. By seeking God's forgiveness and by trusting that Jesus paid the price for us when He died on the cross we are made righteous. It is also clear that we must respond to this gift of grace by living righteous lives. God freely gives us unconditional love, total acceptance, complete forgiveness, membership into His family, and life with Him forever, and we respond by living in the way He desires.

The idea that Jesus' death made us 'righteous' before God is confirmed in numerous places in the Bible. It is prophesied in

Isaiah 53:5–6 and in Jeremiah 31:33–34, referred to by Jesus Himself in Mark 10:45 and implied through the words of the Lord's Supper (Matthew 26:26–29; Mark 14:24; Luke 22:17–23). Later it is also clearly taught by Paul (for example in Romans 3:21–26; 10:3–4; Philippians 3:9).

The notion that the free gift of a righteous status with God comes with a responsibility is also clear in the Bible. When admonishing Pharisees and Sadducees who came to be baptised, John the Baptist says: 'Produce fruit in keeping with repentance . . . The axe is already at the root of the trees, and every tree that does not produce good fruit will be cut down and thrown into the fire' (Matthew 3:8, 10). In the Sermon on the Mount Jesus Himself says: '. . . let your light shine before men, that they may see your good deeds and praise your Father in heaven. Do not think that I have come to abolish the Law or the Prophets; I have not come to abolish them but to fulfil them' (Matthew 5:16–17). His brother James, who later became a leader of the Jerusalem church, also made this point: '. . . faith by itself, if it is not accompanied by action, is dead' (James 2:17). Clearly, after accepting forgiveness and our new status in life, we must put into practice our change of heart through the way we live. Rather than there being a conflict between faith and works, we can see that they actually complement one another and are intricately intertwined.

To see how these two aspects of righteousness work together, let's consider what it means to be a king. Of course, a king is a person who has been granted the right to rule, but it is also someone who *actually* rules. In other words, it is someone who has the title 'king', and who also takes action. A king in name only would soon be superseded, as happened at the beginning of 1936. King George IV died and his son took the title of King Edward VIII, but he was never crowned, and by the end of the year he had also abdicated the throne. In any list of British monarchs, he is considered 'the king who never really was'. After all, it's not enough to have a title or status; it must actually be lived out. In the same way, a marriage which existed in name only would soon be considered null and void. What use is a wedding if the two people within the marriage do not behave as if they are married?

So we can see that righteousness comprises two interlinked components. On the one hand, it's about being called into a relationship with God. On the other, it means living out the implications of that relationship. It must begin, as the first beatitudes remind us, with us realising that we are poor in spirit and mourning over that fact. From that point we do the only thing we can do in those circumstances: we accept God's offer of free forgiveness in Jesus. Yet, as the New Testament makes abundantly clear, this forgiveness does not come by itself or in a vacuum. We are adopted into God's family so that we can now know Him, not as a distant and feared Lord, but as a loving Father. We are also given the gift of His Holy Spirit to assist us to become what we should be. In summary, we have a new righteousness based on forgiveness, which puts us into a new relationship with God. Adopted into the family of God, we are able to act as part of His family, with the help of the Holy Spirit.

It's important to note that this view of righteousness has not changed throughout the Bible, as some people mistakenly believe. (They say that the Old Testament preaches that we are saved by works, while the New Testament focuses on being saved through faith.) In fact, there are great parallels in the Old and New Testament concepts of righteousness. In the Old Testament God called a people by grace and those people then did – or were supposed to do – good things *because* they were God's people. The New Testament pattern is that God calls a people by grace and these people do good things because they are God's people. In other words, there's no great fundamental change. What *did* change was the way in which righteousness was established and also the limitations on who could be made righteous. In the Old Testament righteousness is established as a result of animal sacrifices and it only applies to the Jewish nation. In the New Testament it's made clear that animal sacrifices are no longer necessary because Jesus Himself was a sacrifice sufficient to make us right with God, and the old limitations of race, region and ritual are broken down.

So as we've seen, righteousness involves *being* right *with* God and *doing* right *for* God. It is a state open to *everybody*, thanks to the sacrifice Jesus made on the cross.

WHAT IT MEANS TO HUNGER AND THIRST FOR RIGHTEOUSNESS

In the developed world of the twenty-first century most people are largely unfamiliar with hunger and thirst. In Jesus' time, real hunger or thirst was ever present, as it still is in the developing, majority world. Life was astonishingly vulnerable and supplies of both food and water could easily become scarce: disease could strike cattle; locusts could ravage crops; rains could fail; and springs could dry up. With no governmental welfare system in place under Roman rule, famine or drought would mean death and disaster. Hence, when Jesus spoke of hunger and thirst, people were all too familiar with the dire weight of these words.

Given this context, Jesus' expression to 'hunger and thirst' told of being possessed of a very deep desire – a longing so powerful as to utterly dominate a person's existence. It was a matter of life and death. At the first pangs of hunger a person is likely to put everything else aside, including money, honour, fame and dignity, in order to eat. A thirsty person is likely to forget all else in the pursuit of water.

In this beatitude Jesus is saying that the blessed are those who desire righteousness more than anything else in their lives. He is referring to people who no longer consider wealth, fortune or pride to be valuable because righteousness is the only thing on their agenda. Clearly, Jesus is not just saying we need to *want* righteousness, but that we need to seek it intensely as though our life depends on it. It does!

If you initially find yourself reacting adversely to the idea of being a wild-eyed fanatic, please try and recognise that we're all driven people – whether we recognise it or not – and that there are limits to a moderate approach. Psychologists suggest that we all crave things such as acceptance, pleasure, possessions and honour. Even if you personally are not susceptible to the destructive drive sometimes seen on television game shows or which pushes some people to work a seventy-hour week, do you ever find yourself doing things for reasons you don't fully understand? Do you ever suffer from restlessness? Do you ever long for possessions, holidays or the opportunity to do things *your* way? Also, please recognise that nothing worth achieving was ever reached without some sort of hungering and thirsting. Few millionaires ever made their money by accident; few Nobel Prize winners earned their awards without sweat and tears; and few best-selling novelists achieved their fame without long, lonely hours at their desk.

In the spiritual realm the same holds true. Without determination, little is achieved. Slavery was not ended by a few dashed-off letters of protest; nations were not transformed by someone creating a few snappy slogans over coffee; tyrannies were not overthrown by a man with a placard walking around for a few minutes. We need the tenacity, perseverance and passion that will drive sustained action. In other words, unless we really *hunger* and *thirst* for righteousness, unrighteousness will triumph. To have good wishes without a burning desire to see good happen is to engage in nothing more than daydreaming.

Despite this, hungering and thirsting for righteousness is something that is sadly unfamiliar to many Christians, especially in the West. We seem to have created a Christianity that can be held at arm's length, which involves an hour or so on Sunday, a few minutes each day in prayer and Bible reading – and very little else. In return we ask little of our faith, except that it keeps us well and wealthy and, like an air bag in our car, it helps in an emergency. One reason why we have found Islamic suicide bombers so unsettling is not so much the bombings themselves – terrible though they are – but because we are deeply disturbed to see people who are entirely motivated by their faith! While they are so serious about their religion they are prepared to die for it, some of us find it hard enough *living* for ours.

If you feel that desire itself is wrong (as many Buddhists do) and that the nearest we can get to happiness lies in getting rid of all our desires, again we need to return to the words of the Bible. Jesus' words in this beatitude indicate not that desires in themselves are wrong but that our yearnings can be misplaced. While longing for happiness can be seen to be a misplaced desire (simply because it can never be fulfilled), Jesus says that we can and should long for righteousness because that desire is good and right. The irony is that if we look for happiness we won't find it but if we seek righteousness instead we will not only find it but also have happiness thrown in as a bonus. As Jesus said, 'Seek the Kingdom of God above all else, and live righteously, and he will give you everything you need' (Matthew 6:33, NLT).

THE PRACTICALITIES

Perhaps the most effective way of pursuing righteousness is to start with ourselves and then move progressively outwards, as if we were going through concentric rings of our life.

Accepting righteousness through grace

The first step towards establishing a right relationship with God involves acknowledging that we have failed God, that we are spiritually bankrupt and that our only hope is to seek out God's righteousness. The only way to do this is to accept Christ as Saviour and Lord because He embodies all righteousness. Accepting Him means engaging in the greatest of exchanges: He takes our wrongdoing (our *un*righteousness) and gives us His righteousness in return. In other words, instead of thinking of Jesus as being a guide to life, we need to recognise the reality, which is that He is *the* life. As Jesus says Himself in John 14:6: 'I am the way and the truth and the life. No one comes to the Father except through me.'

The idea that Jesus is the embodiment of righteousness is not just a pleasing, sentimental fancy but also a concept that runs through the whole Bible. In the Old Testament book of Jeremiah we read about the Messiah, who is to come: '"The days are coming," declares the LORD, "when I will raise up to David a righteous Branch, a King who will reign wisely and do what is just and right in the land. In his days Judah will be saved and Israel will live in safety. This is the name by which he will be called: The LORD Our Righteousness"' (Jeremiah 23:5–6). In other words, the Messiah was to be the personification of righteousness. Paul confirms that Jesus was this king when he wrote: 'God made him who had no sin to be sin for us, so that in him we might become the righteousness of God' (2 Corinthians 5:21). He also wrote: '. . . if Christ is in you, your body is dead because of sin, yet your spirit is alive because of righteousness' (Romans 8:10). In other words, by becoming a Christian we become so linked to Jesus that His righteousness becomes our own. When God looks at us He doesn't see our sin, but the righteousness of Jesus instead.

Theologians call this 'imputed righteousness' and the contemporary American preacher John Piper writes in one of his sermons:

> I linger over this issue of the imputed righteousness of God in Christ because when I stand by your bed in the hour of your death, I want to be able to look down into your face and remind you of the most comforting words in all the world, and have you rejoice with solid Biblical understanding in what I mean when I say: 'Remember, Christ is your righteousness. Christ is your righteousness. Your righteousness is in heaven. It's the same yesterday today and forever. It doesn't get better when your faith is strong. It doesn't get worse when your faith is weak. It is perfect. It is Christ. Look away from yourself. Rest in him. Lean on him.' (Sermon, 17 October 1999)

Have you accepted God's gift of righteousness?

Examining our righteousness in action

As followers of Christ, we need to go beyond God's legal verdict of 'Not guilty' and actually live out a righteous life. A summary of what it means to live out righteousness is given in the Old Testament, in Micah 6:8: 'He has showed you, O man, what is good. And what does the LORD require of you? To act justly and to love mercy and to walk humbly with your God.' (I wrote a whole book – *Walking with God* – just on that verse!) Micah's words are echoed in the Beatitudes: acting, loving and walking mercifully are key elements of righteousness.

Of course, it's easier to say these words than to enact them in one's life. It's so much easier to turn the spotlight onto other people's lives and find fault with them, rather than with ourselves. It can even be extraordinarily satisfying concentrating on the failings of our neighbours, the Prime Minister, the President of the

United States or some tyrant miles away. After all, as someone once said, criticism is indirect self-praise. However, we would do well to remember the wise saying that reminds us that pointing a finger at someone else inevitably involves pointing four fingers back at ourselves.

In order to examine ourselves we could perhaps ask a few questions: Are we personally honest? Are we fair in our dealings with others? Do we constantly strive to be kind, giving and helpful? Is our prime concern in life to be a blessing to others? Are we glad when evil is frustrated? Do we delight in the truth? Do we grieve over moral bankruptcy? Do we bring not only our concerns but also our thanks to God in prayer? Do we come before God dissatisfied with who we are, seeking His forgiveness? Is there a real living faith in our lives? The list of questions we need to ask ourselves could well continue.

One of the problems with trying to live out any sort of personal righteousness is that we now live in a culture in which ethics are not very high on anybody's agenda. The result is that we often find ourselves mixing with people who in a previous generation would have been called 'rogues'. You know what I mean: the sort of people who openly admit to cheating on their tax returns, who manifestly inflate their travel expenses, who flippantly brag about their recent sexual escapades, who go out of their way to bend and break every possible rule. These people may quite openly throw their weight around and are loudmouthed, if not downright bullying, to people around them. The real danger with being close to such people is not that we become like them but that we consider ourselves vastly superior to them. Associating with people like this might prompt us to pray: 'Don't talk to *me* about morality! What about X with his hard disk full of illegally copied movies? What about Y who is openly messing around with someone else's partner? What about Z and his ruthless campaign to get the boss's job?'

In order to focus our attention on ourselves we would be wise to read through the Gospels and compare ourselves, not with people around us, but with Jesus Christ Himself. If we really want to compare ourselves with anybody else, it should be with people who are definitely holier than us. If, to use the words of the first beatitude, we come away feeling poor in spirit, then so much the better. Above all, whoever we compare ourselves to, we need to remember that morality, like charity, needs to begin at home. After all, this and the other beatitudes are personal challenges more than anything else.

Developing righteous relationships

The final essential step is to focus on building righteous relationships with everybody with whom we come into contact. After all, as well as relating to how we get right with God, the Beatitudes are also concerned with how we live our lives publicly.

In case you question the desirability of having righteousness in the world, consider for a moment what would result if everyone were righteous:

> The rich would seek to help the poor.

> Senior women would be spoilt for choice as people queued up to help them cross roads.

> Companies would return profits to customers.

> People would trust announcements made by the government.

> The world's poor would be fed on the money that is usually spent on the military.

> The police would have the best sports teams because there'd be nothing left for them to do.

The divorce courts would be empty.

All burglar alarm, security and surveillance firms would go bust.

Many newspapers would go out of circulation because they'd no longer have anything to gossip about.

Does that make righteousness seem worthwhile? Righteousness is frequently little more than fairness, honesty, kindness and decency. Let's try another angle. One of the few Hebrew words widely known today is the word *shalom*. It is normally translated as 'peace', but actually it is linked with the idea of righteousness. For a society to have *shalom* is for it to be a society where righteousness reigns. It would be a society in which there is no wrongdoing, no injustice, no unfairness and no prejudice.

Picture, for a moment, an image of several concentric circles. Think of righteousness as spiralling outwards from the centre, the locus of your personal righteousness, to your family, your local community, your town, your country and even the whole wide world.

Think first about your family. Can you help bring righteousness there? Is there someone who needs to be reconciled with someone else? Is there some injustice to do with the past that must be addressed? Is there some old hurt that needs to be resolved? Almost every family has wounds that need to be healed. Resolving them might be as simple as writing a letter or making a phone call. Yet we must not only deal with the past, but also the present and the future. Where there is a persisting evil, we must work for it to end and not return. Lies, verbal abuse, angry words and humiliation must end. Righteousness must be the rule in future relationships. But be under no illusion; this will not be easy. After all, you may need to think carefully about how to stop someone who is persistently undermining another member of the family or being abusive. Would it be appropriate to deal with it on the spot each time it occurs? Do you instead need to take that person aside and say some difficult words of truth? Do you need to support the victim? Or do you need to take even more drastic action so as to protect more vulnerable people in the family? Remember the top of your list of priority at all times should be the question: Is there anything I can change in my own personal behaviour to help the situation on a day-to-day basis, so as to bring in more righteousness?

After considering your family in this way, allow yourself to spiral outwards to your local community. Think about the people you work with, play among and live with as neighbours. Here too we must long for righteousness to prevail. Why not ask God to show you what urgently needs to be put right? Hungering and thirsting for righteousness may, rather inconveniently, force us to take a stand. For instance, it's very common now for many organisations to be slightly 'economical with the truth' when it comes to talking about the virtues of their product. Righteousness may mean that someone has to walk into the office of the boss, the chief accountant, or the marketing manager and say, 'I'm sorry, we can't do this. It's just not true.' Perhaps if some kind of financial scam occurs, instead of saying, 'Oh, it's nothing much – just what everyone does,' we now need to say, 'No. Count me out.' What about the many situations in which firms hire part-time labour on the basis that they do not have to pay pensions, so if the economy takes a downturn such staff can be let go without problems? Is that righteousness in action? You may find dealing with such things hard, but I can guarantee that the search for that elusive thing we call 'happiness' will be even more difficult if you fail to deal with an issue of righteousness at your very own back door.

Let's continue spiralling outwards. What about the street or block of flats where you live? What would it mean for the light of righteousness to flood your neighbourhood? What about your town? And please don't just pick on those obvious visible targets: the youths drinking rowdily on the square, the speeding drivers, the fly-tippers and the prostitutes. Some of the worst evil goes on beneath the surface, carried out in neat, clean offices by quietly spoken, impeccably dressed, well-educated men and women – tax evasion; employment of immigrants at illegal rates; the diversion of grants; the defrauding of the elderly; the fixing of 'overheads' with the council or the government; and the bending of planning laws to name a few. People who appear to be decent members of society often carry out these unrighteous actions. Yet however well disguised, evil is still evil. If we are to hunger and thirst for righteousness we need to take a stand against these offences.

Now lift your eyes higher and look beyond your immediate surroundings to the wider world – your final concentric circle. There you will see so much that is unjust. Let me challenge you to pick up any newspaper and put a tick against an article that deals with some form of wrong or injustice. You will find yourself covering the newspaper with ticks. Let me list some topics at random:

Tax laws are manipulated so that many who earn millions effectively remain untaxed, while others struggle to pay their bills.

Major corporations manage to bulldoze their way through the laws of weak states by using bribery and corruption.

Companies that produce cigarettes and alcohol push their products on people in 'the developing markets' who really don't need them.

Managers of firms give themselves massive bonuses while cheating the consumer and laying off the 'little people', who keep the company in business.

Arms traders make enormous profits trading all kinds of weapons that will be used to prop up despotic regimes or those with criminal intent.

Refugees roam from place to place, often in flight from an oppressive regime, in hopes of finding someone to welcome them.

The priceless resources of our natural environment are squandered by a tiny minority of wealthy people.

The wealthy manage to afford lawyers, while the poor are left to defend themselves.

Considering these and other unrighteous practices, it's vital that we consider what we can do on a personal level, within our social environment. If we fail to deal with our own unrighteousness then we will be unhappy hypocrites always lecturing others from a position of weakness. And if our focus is too narrow – looking only at ourselves, and not our family, our neighbourhoods, our places of work and the wider world – then we will effectively become armchair moralists.

Being righteous on a personal level really can make a difference. It's extraordinary how, despite the vast forces of politics, culture and economics, history so often revolves around individuals. Individual men and women can start wars and stop them and it's often solitary figures who are responsible for beginning or ending revolutions. Individuals can lead a nation over the precipice into utter disaster, or they can lead them away from the brink of oblivion. We *can* make a difference. One man or woman's stand for righteousness can avert disaster.

In case you still feel it's a tall order to do anything yourself, let me remind you that Jesus doesn't say 'Blessed *are* the righteous'. Instead, he blesses those who *seek* to achieve righteousness, so don't worry about failing. There will be many in heaven who did not achieve much in the way of righteousness that can be quantified or measured. According to Jesus, the fact that they hungered and thirsted for righteousness is what really counts.

THE BLESSING

The blessing for us when we hunger and thirst for righteousness is wonderfully simple: we are told 'we will be filled'. Our hunger and thirst will be appeased and we will feel satisfied.

Living in our Western culture of fast food and microwave meals, where food is often seen as nothing more than fuel, we need to pay particular attention to this idea of being 'filled'. Jesus doesn't simply say, 'they will have something to eat,' but that we will be *filled*. In other words, our hunger and thirst will actually come to an end.

As is so often the case in the New Testament, there may be far more to this than actually meets the eye. It's likely that Jesus is referring back to the Old Testament, as He does repeatedly else-where during His teaching. This makes sense because while neither Jesus nor His audience would have been 'widely read' they would certainly have been very familiar with the part of the Bible Christians call the Old Testament (the Jewish 'Torah'). They would have known whole chunks of the Old Testament by heart and one section they might have thought of at this point would have been the book of Isaiah. Two important passages from this book talk about food and drink. These passages look forward to the end of time and to the coming of the kingdom.

On this mountain the LORD Almighty will prepare a feast of rich food for all peoples, a banquet of aged wine – the best of meats and the finest of wines. On this mountain he will destroy the shroud that enfolds all peoples, the sheet that covers all nations; he will swallow up death for ever. The Sovereign LORD will wipe away the tears from all faces; he will remove the disgrace of his people from all the earth. The LORD has spoken. In that day they will say, 'Surely this is our God; we trusted in him, and he saved us. This is the LORD, we trusted in him; let us rejoice and be glad in his salvation.' (Isaiah 25:6–9)

Come, all you who are thirsty, come to the waters; and you who have no money, come, buy and eat! Come, buy wine and milk without money and without cost. Why spend money on what is not bread, and your labour on what does not satisfy? Listen, listen to me, and eat what is good, and your soul will delight in the richest of fare. (Isaiah 55:1–2)

In other words it seems likely that in this beatitude Jesus is referring to some of the prophecies about the Messiah. The idea of being filled means being satisfied in this life, and in the next. Jesus promises this fulfilling with absolute confidence. Those who yearn for God above all else will certainly have all their desires granted.

TO SUM UP

This fourth beatitude refers to the goal we need to have for our lives and the determination we need in order to reach it. As we've seen, the goal itself is righteousness. First of all we need to confirm our own right status with God, then we need to strive to improve this sad and troubled world. Jesus makes it clear that we mustn't approach this goal lazily – our desire to reach it must be as strong as the hunger and thirst of a dying person.

Here we must come back to the title of this book. I suspect by now you must have wondered if I had forgotten all about it.

Thinking back to the quest for happiness we are reminded here that only a search for righteousness will really quench our thirst. Any attempts to find happiness through possessions, power or pleasure will inevitably cheat us, in that they will be like drinking salt water – they intensify thirst, rather than diminishing it. This shouldn't come as a surprise because most people are aware that seeking happiness usually results in a feeling of anti-climax. You know the kind of thing: you save for months for a wonderful holiday; you prepare for it as if it was a military campaign. Yet even if all goes well, it is a near certainty that on the flight or ferry back, you will realise it was a disappointment. The happiness you sought will have somehow slipped through your fingers once more. If you seek happiness in a new home you will soon find yourself lying awake in bed, staring at the ceiling, grappling with the realisation that the new house isn't going to deliver the lasting bliss you hoped it might. Or perhaps you wait and pray for years that God would send you a husband or wife and you finally achieve your dream of marriage. However, the day inevitably comes when your spouse lets you down and you are sent once again asking for more.

So widespread is the recognition that our desires are rarely (if ever) fulfilled that some people become hopeless cynics. They scoff at the very word 'happiness'. For some, cynicism is so deeply entrenched that all desire has been abandoned. These people only dare to hope to survive from one day to the next.

This beatitude flies in the face of this attitude. It tells us not only that it's good to have a desire, but also that it's likely to be fulfilled if it's a desire for righteousness. One Greek myth sums it up by portraying a king – King Tantalus – in an eternal state of punishment. He was made to stand in a pool of water under a fruit tree with low branches but he couldn't reach the fruit from the branches to satisfy his hunger, or the water to satisfy his thirst. It's easy to see how this is a dramatic illustration of one of the characteristics of hell: the presence of hunger or thirst that cannot ever be satisfied. Here in the blessing of this beatitude we have heaven's counterpart – those who hunger and thirst for righteousness will be filled. What greater happiness can there be than this?

5

Be Merciful

Blessed are the merciful,
for they will be shown mercy.
(Matthew 5:7)

A NATURAL PROGRESSION

This fifth beatitude builds naturally on the first four. Picture the Beatitudes as a beautiful, fruitful tree. The first two beatitudes correspond to two essential roots, which keep our lives deeply anchored in the rich soil of God's grace. One root is our need to acknowledge our guilt before God and the other root is our need to grieve over that same unworthiness. The next two beatitudes can be viewed as referring to the way in which the tree grows. The third beatitude, which upholds humility, makes the point that we must allow the growth of our lives to be shaped by God. The fourth beatitude (which talks of our need to hunger and thirst for righteousness) refers to the direction in which we are to grow. As trees must rise up towards the light, so we must grow in the direction of righteousness. To varying degrees, these first four beatitudes are primarily God focused, although of course the fourth beatitude – focusing on righteousness – does force us to look at our relationship with the outside world.

THE NEED TO RELATE

When we reach the fifth beatitude, the focus is even more strongly on our relationships with others, on the branches of the tree, which need to reach out and bear fruit. Does it seem odd to you that blessing (or happiness) comes from getting involved with other people? Nowadays, it's as if most people assume that happiness can only be obtained alone or by focusing on 'things'. This attitude perhaps explains why relationships are not as prioritised today as they were in the past. The buzz in our conversations can often centre on bargains on eBay, the latest computer technology, the best holiday location, the wider-screen television or the newest clothes. To put it very simply, 'stuff' has become so important in our lives that people have become marginalised.

Intertwined with this trend is a move towards what we might call 'isolationism'. Many people leave work and commute home enclosed in a private world of sound from headphones or the car stereo before entering their home and closing the door behind them. Inside, on their own, they spend solitary evenings watching television, surfing the web or listening to music. Their relationships with other people are often distant, and the result is that they never need to display any characteristics that might be described as 'merciful'. When people do make contact with others they tend to opt out at the first sign of difficulty. I mention this here because mercy, in its very nature, deals with the hard side of relationships. You don't really need mercy when everything is going well. So even before we have considered in any way what it means to have mercy you need to be forewarned that it means a commitment to dealing with other human beings – sometimes to the point of pain and even anguish.

WHAT IS MERCY?

It's all very well Jesus telling us to be merciful, but what's He talking about exactly? Sometimes the most familiar words hold the biggest surprises because they're overused, mostly in idiomatic phrases, instead of being considered alone. Mercy – an everyday, commonplace word – is no exception, and what I want to do is explore it as deeply as possible. Mercy is forgiveness and kindness motivated by love. Mercy is compassion in action: practical compassion, applied compassion. As we shall see, rightly understood, mercy is wider, harder, rarer and more precious than most of us ever suppose.

Mercy is wide-ranging

We usually think of the word 'mercy' in dramatic terms. We may think of a 'mercy mission', perhaps involving rescue planes and helicopters urgently setting out to try and save lives. We might also envisage specific 'acts of mercy': perhaps a judge pardoning a man condemned to death or an aid worker cradling an emaciated baby. An 'errand of mercy' might come to mind – an awkward, painful visit to the bereaved after some tragedy. Or we might think of a 'mercy dash', such as an urgent, cross-country drive to the bedside of a patient whose life is fast fading away. We may even consider the complex and tragic issues behind so-called 'mercy killings'. While these might all include use of the word 'mercy' I would like to suggest that, in the context of this beatitude, they might be profoundly misleading.

Here, as elsewhere in the Beatitudes, we tend to take the characteristic that Jesus refers to and amplify it into a dramatic and spectacular form – a form which is actually distorted. For example, we see 'meekness' as referring to someone whose manner is so self-effacing and retiring that their neighbours don't know they exist. We assume that 'being a peacemaker' refers to the type of person the Secretary General of the United Nations might regularly phone for advice. When we think of a person who 'hungers and thirsts for righteousness' we imagine a figure comparable to Nelson Mandela. So when we come to this beatitude on being merciful, our minds may immediately conjure up either a noble figure along the lines of Mother Teresa or some horrific challenge to do with life or death.

The curious thing is that by making these phrases apply only to special people in unusual situations, we actually undermine the Beatitudes and make them so narrow and specific that they appear to be irrelevant to us personally. Our tendency to exaggerate the meaning of the individual words Jesus uses makes them seem utterly unattainable, which makes us feel they must be impractical. The net result is that we sadly end up ignoring their very practical, wide-ranging implications in our own modest situation. It's a bit like being advised by your doctor to take more exercise. If you tell yourself that you're being asked to run a marathon you'll probably reject the advice. By exaggerating the advice, you make it seem so impractical that ignoring it is the only sensible approach.

The fact of the matter is that while mercy does extend to the highest heights, much of it is simply a very down-to-earth part of our everyday lives. It can include such ordinary and commonplace things as kindness, forgiveness, compassion, sympathy and caring. While it can relate to the situations that result in the tabloid headlines – 'Mother forgives son's killer', 'Firm lets debtors off' and 'Top doctor to work in African slum' – it will usually involve very ordinary actions. These might include writing a letter of consolation, holding your tongue at a difficult moment out of respect for someone else's feelings, passing on a few words of encouragement or even giving a friendly smile. Put simply, mercy is a great summary word for all those things that make life bearable in our relationships with other people. It encompasses the expression of the greatest of all Christian virtues: love.

Mercy can be hard

Having seen that mercy is a more everyday virtue than we might imagine, we also need to note that it is actually much harder to apply than we might initially think. Being merciful means doing something with a personal *cost*. In some cases where time, money or energy is involved, the cost may be obvious. We might give money to charity, help a neighbour mow their lawn or rewrite a colleague's badly prepared report. It usually costs more than that, though. In being merciful, we come alongside people and often reach down to the level of those we are helping. The mercy we show towards others when we lift them up effectively reduces the gap between us so we inevitably take a knock in status.

In many situations, ranging from the home to the military, the law courts to the classroom, fear is a vital tool in maintaining discipline and getting something done. While a merciless attitude makes other people apprehensive and respectful, one which shows mercy undermines this fear and invites familiarity, if not contempt. A friend told me about a teacher who said his secret for keeping discipline was to find an excuse, however trivial, for losing his temper in the first week. Apparently, this kept the children scared for the rest of the year. Being merciful in the classroom, as elsewhere, means running the risk that you might be considered a 'soft touch', a 'pushover' or just simply weak. Being merciful can at times undermine your authority and status in the world's eyes. In the hard game of life, showing mercy may appear to be a bad tactical mistake.

As if this weren't enough, being merciful might also adversely affect our relationships in other ways because it forces other people into a different, perhaps humiliating position. In other words, the person who is on the receiving end of mercy may feel forced into a situation where he or she owes the merciful person a favour.

Showing mercy is also difficult because it presents us with the almost irresistible temptation to gloat. If, after showing mercy, we continually allude to it we are actually not showing mercy, but manipulating other people. Clearly, mercy must be given with no strings attached. Of course, this is in stark contrast to the way in which, in many cultures including that in which Jesus lived, people accumulate mental lists of those who owe them favours.

Finally, it's important to note that mercy is not something which we can make another person *earn* or negotiate for. The whole point of mercy is that it is a gift to those who do not deserve it.

Mercy is rare

In most cultures, mercy is a relatively rare commodity. In all too many societies, you hear sad tales of how some relatively minor grievance sparked a reprisal, which in turn triggered a larger re-taliation, which was greeted by retribution on a yet greater scale. And so the matter continued until all the parties were exhausted or dead. A society in which mercy is undervalued is one in which vendettas and feuds tend to proliferate. In fact, in such societies you may find that if some individual asks for mercy to be shown to a wrongdoer, the community as a whole may reject the request for fear that it will show they are weak. It is all too common to hear of families or communities who promote a tough image of themselves. 'Don't mess with us or else' is their unwritten motto.

I think there is some basis for concluding that, in the twenty-first century, mercy is something of an endangered species world-wide. Mercy faces many threats. One is what we may summarise as 'the market economy', a principle that dominates in most of the world. This view advocates that every action must make a profit. Imagine a firm faced with an increase in costs where a manager wanted to withhold the increase from consumers. Market forces dictate that profits must remain unaffected, so the increase is passed on anyway. Mercy may just be too costly.

Another threat to mercy is the widespread acceptance of what has been called 'social Darwinism'. The concept of 'the survival of the fittest' or 'the law of the jungle' has become widely accepted, not just as a scientific theory, but as a way that society operates. Mercy, it is assumed, is for wimps and losers. 'May God have mercy upon my enemies, because I won't,' is what the famous American General George Patton said. Many would echo such sentiments well beyond the battlefield. (Patton was an Episcopalian – a member of The Church of Our Savior, San Gabriel, where you will find a bronze statue of him in the rose garden and a stained glass window of him in his tank!) Business managers are advised to be tough because they are told that in business they will be prey or predator, killer or killed and that mercy will be a threat to their very survival. Ironically many businesses (for example, those run by Quakers) have thrived despite an entirely different approach.

Still another threat to mercy comes from the widespread use and influence of computers in almost every area of society. Digital systems know nothing of mercy and their ability to transform human beings into anonymous strings of data is devastating. Computers will accept no excuses and will offer no sympathy. Speed cameras, for example, do not distinguish between the reckless joy rider and a person who is desperate to get to the bedside of a dying relative. It is not just the machines themselves that are merciless – by their very nature they exert an influence on the people who use them. As soon as people become numbers, it becomes all too easy to treat them as items to be relocated, processed or even disposed of, at will.

A final threat to mercy comes from the current climate of 'demands and rights' in which the increasing reaction to injustice or misfortune involves finding a lawyer. In the past, someone might have rushed in to help at the scene of an accident, or in the case of an unfortunate business incident. Now people hesitate, wondering if they might become liable for something or vulnerable to being sued.

In the light of these factors, it's hardly surprising that mercy has become such a rarity. Living in the modern world has become like surfing on high waves: if you stay on the board it's great, but if you fall off you quickly drown. What may also be surprising, though, is the fact that the world Jesus lived in was very similar. If anything it was even more merciless. People could easily be bought or sold and life was literally cheap. The Romans, whom you may be sure did not gain their massive empire by merciful actions, thought that mercy was a disease of the soul. A Roman citizen could kill a slave, a young child and even a troublesome wife. Their practice of public crucifixion, the most brutal, shameful and protracted form of execution, typifies their attitude to mercy. However, even in the face of all this, Jesus upheld mercy.

From this beatitude it's clear that Jesus was capable of envisioning a society having mercy at the forefront of its value system, and we must do so too. Since mercy embodies such a rare approach, we need to recognise that it is something that has to be taught and learned.

Mercy is exceedingly precious

As you are perhaps beginning to see (if you hadn't done so beforehand), a merciful approach is truly worth nurturing. A merciful approach is perhaps the only one capable of turning the tide in society. Mercy encourages forgiveness for the wrongdoer, consolation for the bereaved, comfort for the lonely and assistance for the poor. Mercy, great and small, is the oil that smoothes the violent and rough machinery of everyday life. It produces smiles of encouragement, encouraging pats on the back, shoulders to cry on and a listening ear. It is that wonderful quality that withholds criticism, that opts out of arguments and that even offers a cup of tea at a time of crisis.

In case you aren't convinced of the importance of mercy, let's do what we've done in previous chapters and consider the opposite. Imagine, if you dare, a work setting, a relationship or even a world in which people are always hard-hearted, unsympathetic and cold – never merciful. Imagine how the weak would be cheated, the frail ridiculed and how anyone different – by nature or choice – would be persecuted. In the last hundred years our world has seen many regimes that have made mercilessness their byword. The mass graveyards they have left behind contain the remains of those they saw as their political opponents, who were socially undesirable or considered somehow racially inferior. If we consider these scenarios, we will soon realise the cruel nature of a world without mercy.

In order to really appreciate the value of mercy it's helpful to imagine a perfect situation. Visualise a villa of great architectural style inhabited by a small group of people gifted with beauty, wit, health and intelligence. Imagine them all sitting around a dining table laden with the finest food and drink, and visualise them gazing out at a sun-drenched vista of unblemished sand, palm trees and endless sea. Listen in to the happy, gentle, lively tone of their conversation. This, we might say, is heaven. Now just take away from that visualisation one small thing: *mercy*. Imagine what would happen. The precise trigger for the heartlessness is irrelevant: it could be a misinterpreted comment, a drop of wine spilt on a dress, a knife put down too noisily. At first slowly, and then with ever-increasing speed, awkwardness would change into annoyance, insinuation would be countered by accusations and irritation would flare up into a row. With nothing to dampen it or stop it, the wit turns to cutting sarcasm, smiles switch to snarls, gentle voices become shrill shouts, faces redden with anger and fists become clenched. Heaven becomes hell. Mercy is not an optional extra in life – it's an essential ingredient.

WHY DO WE NEED MERCY?

Very few of Jesus' hearers would have been surprised by His praising mercy as the virtue that ought to dominate our relationships with others. Here as ever, Jesus did not speak in a vacuum – He completed and fulfilled the moral teaching of the Old Testament rather than replacing it (Matthew 5:17–18). Mercy is one of the great themes, perhaps *the* great theme, of the Old Testament and through Jesus' teaching, its central place continues into the New Testament.

We're all guilty

To understand the role mercy plays we first need to stand back and see the position of the human race and our relationship with God. The Bible minces no words: it makes it clear that as a species and as individuals we have all broken God's laws. I suspect that deep in our hearts we all realise this but look for a range of excuses to deny the reality of it.

One method we have for avoiding the challenge of God's laws is to question whether they are really rules at all. We might reclassify them as 'guidelines' and see the Ten Commandments not as God's rules for existence, but as some sort of idealistic advisory code. We suggest they are just rules for an ideal world, which it would be nice to keep, if only life were a little more perfect. Another mental trick we might use to dodge the idea that God is a lawgiver to whom we are answerable, is to hope that He might not even notice us. Still another mental dodge is to imagine that God doesn't really mind. While hopelessly blurring images of Santa Claus and the Almighty God we conjure up the image of someone who is far too genial to bother getting worked up about actually enforcing rights and wrongs. 'After all,' we think, 'He's a nice bloke. God is love, isn't He?' Finally, if we're *really* desperate we claim we really aren't as bad as some people. *We* have not committed mass murder, *we* haven't abused any children and *we* have certainly not defrauded anybody. Compared to everyone else, we conclude, we're innocent.

These thoughts are a bit like going just too fast past a traffic camera, seeing the flash and dreaming up various 'saving graces' – hoping there was no film in the camera, that the authorities will be too busy to bother, or that our own speeding ticket will get lost in the red tape. And none of these excuses align with the Bible's message. Repeatedly, the Bible tells us that God's rules need to be observed and it provides us with plenty of stories to indicate that ignoring or breaking them has consequences. The Bible also repeatedly points out that God does see everything and that one day there will indeed be a day of accounting for what we have or haven't done with our lives. Of course, the Bible also points out that God is a God of justice and righteousness who cares very much that justice will prevail in His universe. As far as the final excuse is concerned, the Bible makes it clear that God's rules are absolute and not relative. It's irrelevant whether or not other people are guilty because the fact is, we're guilty ourselves.

In short, we all badly need mercy. Every single one of us.

We need God's help

If the Bible is clear on our problem it is also clear on the solution. God deals mercifully with our guilt. Although the Old Testament God is often depicted as a vengeful figure full of wrath, this is a caricature. One statement about God that occurs repeatedly throughout the Old Testament, almost word for word, describes God as full of 'compassion and mercy . . . slow to anger and filled with unfailing love and faithfulness' (Exodus 34:6; Psalms 86:15; 103:8; 145:8; Joel 2:13; Jonah 4:2, NLT). In other words, when the Old Testament Jews defined God they saw His mercy as being very central to who He was. In fact, a key Old Testament word is the Hebrew word *hesed*, which we struggle to translate into English, but which might be rendered 'mercy', 'love' or 'loving kindness'. It is the sort of love that expects little in return, and is shown towards people who are afflicted. One of the most striking psalms is Psalm 136, where every one of the twenty-six verses includes the refrain 'His love endures for ever' – with some translations (e.g. the King James) translating 'love' as 'mercy'.

In one sense, the New Testament continues the Old Testament teaching on God's mercy – in 2 Corinthians 1:3 we see God referred to as 'our merciful Father' (NLT). In another sense, though, everything is turned upside down. I think if you had asked an Old Testament Jew how God was merciful, he or she would have included something along the lines of, 'The LORD accepts sacrifices as alternatives for punishing us for our sin.' God was considered merciful because He had found a way of forgiving people by allowing them to sacrifice animals. In the New Testament something far greater is revealed: in Jesus Christ, God Himself becomes the sacrifice for our sins. Instead of animals being regularly sacrificed in the Temple, God, in the person of Jesus, dies one horrible death. In the New Testament the anonymous writer of the letter to the Hebrews expresses it like this: '. . . now he has appeared once for all at the end of the ages to do away with sin by the sacrifice of himself. Just as man is destined to die once, and after that to face judgment, so Christ was sacrificed once to take away the sins of many people; and he will appear a second time, not to bear sin, but to bring salvation to those who are waiting for him' (Hebrews 9:26–28). The whole sacrificial system of the Old Testament is seen as something that foreshadowed and symbolised Christ's death on the cross.

This enormous act of forgiveness clearly demonstrates God's merciful nature. However, we should note that the mercy He shows is not easily given. It is costly because it was bought with blood, so it should not be treated lightly. It's important to note this in the context of this beatitude, because there is often a misunderstanding. Some people have looked at 'blessed are the merciful for they shall receive mercy' and seen in it the prospect of a deal. They say, in effect, 'If I am merciful, God will also be merciful. God will repay me in the same currency as I use for others.' A similar problem verse exists in the Lord's Prayer, 'Forgive us our sins, as we forgive those who sin against us.' Taken either separately or together, people have assumed that these indicate that if we show mercy or forgiveness God will look favourably upon us to the same degree that we have looked upon others. Such a view goes right against the traditional Christian view that God's grace and forgiveness comes to us first. It is not given in *response* to our merciful acts, but as a step in the necessary process of reconciliation to bring us back into a relationship with God.

In fact, when we look at these verses in context, the view that we can save ourselves by acts of goodness and mercy doesn't stand up, for three important reasons:

God's mercy would not be 'mercy' if it was given in response to our own mercy – it would be a wage. In that case, the best the Bible might offer would be to celebrate God's fairness by giving us a reasonable rate of exchange. No, all the Old Testament language of mercy highlights a single simple fact: God takes the initiative in healing our broken relationship with Him. His mercy comes first. The mercy we personally give is secondary and constitutes a poor imitation of the real thing.

It's clear that this beatitude is not talking about forgiveness because Jesus here is talking to His disciples. He is addressing people who have already come into a right relationship with Himself, already knowing His forgiveness. This in fact follows the biblical pattern, which involves someone 'becoming' a Christian before they are able to 'behave' like one. In other words, we become God's people first and consequently try to live as God's people.

If we had only broken a small number of God's laws then we might be able to work out a deal with God. The problem, though, is that we haven't broken just one or two laws – we've broken them all in almost every possible way. If God were to forgive us on the basis that we forgave others we would be in trouble. The fact is that even the best of us only engage in a partial and limited forgiveness. Yet such a cautious and qualified forgiveness is quite inadequate to cover failings on our scale. Only flawless and complete forgiveness is capable of covering over all the wrong things that we've done. We need a limitless mercy perfect in breadth and vast in depth – i.e. the type of mercy that can only come from God.

You can probably see here the way in which a Bible-based Christianity has proved itself to be very irritating to those who try to be religious. It says that all our attempts to earn mercy are self-defeating. The only way to come to God is to admit failings and enter that most humiliating plea of 'guilty'.

WHY DO WE NEED TO BE MERCIFUL OURSELVES?

I can imagine that some people might prefer to conclude this chapter here. After all, we've found out that God has offered His mercy freely to us and all we have to do is accept it by trusting in Jesus Christ. Yet this is really only the beginning of the message of Christianity.

It's an inevitable part of being a Christian

We need to do more than just sit around rejoicing in our forgiveness and celebrating that God has rescued us. In fact, the Bible makes it clear that God's mercy in Christ is shown to us not just so we can stay as we are, but also so that we can attain our full potential. The New Testament teaches that once we have become part of God's family through accepting His free forgiveness we are to work at acquiring the family resemblance and become like Christ. Specifically in the context of this beatitude, we are shown mercy so that we might show mercy to others. This is crucial because experiencing God's mercy inevitably makes us merciful ourselves.

Jesus said so!

One of the most famous examples of Jesus explaining the importance of mercy is the story of the Good Samaritan (Luke 10:25–37). In this story a Samaritan (one of a group of people despised by Jewish people for having dubious racial status) is travelling on the notorious Jerusalem to Jericho road when he stumbles across the victim of a violent robbery: a half-naked, injured man. No doubt aware that the wounded man is a Jew, the Samaritan shows him mercy in the most practical of ways: he gives him first aid, takes him somewhere safe to recover and even pays what today we would call the medical costs. The tale clearly illustrates what it means to show practical mercy. The point it makes in particular is that it is not enough to show kindness only to one's friends or family – which should be automatic – but that it's necessary to help a stranger in need, even when this demands a personal cost. The Samaritan must have realised that, given the depth of hatred between Jews and his people, he'd never receive any thanks if this man did recover. This is true of other kinds of mercy too. It is given without consideration for what may ensue, without any interest in gaining friends or influence, but simply in the knowledge that it is the right thing to do.

We need to follow Jesus' example

Jesus was the perfect model of mercy – He shows deep care for all, whether they are rich or poor, male or female, old or young – even Jew, Greek or Roman. This is nowhere clearer than at the crucifixion, which Christians have always seen as being the ultimate demonstration of God's mercy. In the four Gospels, Jesus is recorded as making seven short statements while nailed to the cross. The statements have traditionally been known as 'The Seven Last Words'. Jesus' followers have always considered them particularly important. (There is a very basic reason for this; those being crucified rarely engage in idle chit-chat!) Of these seven sayings, the first three are to do with mercy.

First Jesus prayed for mercy on those involved in the crucifixion, saying, 'Father, forgive them, for they don't know what they are doing' (Luke 23:34, NLT).

Jesus also gave a statement of forgiveness and hope to the repentant criminal being crucified next to Him: 'I assure you, today you will be with me in paradise' (Luke 23:43, NLT).

Finally, we are told that Jesus turned to His mother and John the disciple in front of the cross and said to His mother, 'Dear woman, here is your son.' And he said to this disciple, 'Here is your mother' (John 19:26–27, NLT). In doing this He ensured that His mother would be looked after in the days ahead.

At a time when a person might normally be expected to be self-absorbed, we find that Jesus was still merciful to others. This is something worth remembering when the task of being merciful seems too hard to put into practice in our own lives.

TIPS FOR A MERCIFUL LIFE

Although the Beatitudes are simple, they are not simplistic. How we live them out demands that we engage in serious thought. Anyone under the illusion that to be a follower of Jesus is an easy option could not be further from the truth. Practising any beatitude requires careful consideration, but this one more than most. There is no doubt that the world has greatly suffered from too little mercy, yet it is also true that some harm has been done by the careless application of mercy. There are cases (probably fewer than you might imagine but nevertheless too many) where people have been allowed through 'mercy' to continue to do things they shouldn't have done. Jesus said that His followers should be as shrewd – possibly as wary – as snakes and as harmless as doves (Matthew 10:16). This is a good rule. In the area of mercy, wisdom and gentleness must go hand in hand. Let me give you a few guidelines for this.

Be wise

If we are to be loving and effective as Christians we must always balance mercy and justice. Sometimes there will be a tension between the two and we must choose which side to emphasise. An obvious point that needs to be made is that although we should strive to have a merciful character and to desire mercy there may be situations in which we are simply not authorised to be merciful. For instance, imagine a judge entrusted by the government to enforce law and order, facing an issue of sentencing. However strongly she might want to show mercy, her task is that ordained by the state and she has no authority to dilute her duty. I have no doubt that she might be able to advise on a course of action in which a plea for mercy could be formally and appropriately submitted but neither she nor we can be merciful to others beyond the scope of our current situation.

We could also consider this in terms of a teacher supervising an exam. However much he might long for a struggling pupil to receive mercy, he cannot waive the rules of the exam board and let the student see the paper in advance. Mercy cannot excuse wrongdoing. Additionally, the word 'mercy' must not be used to sweeten the unacceptable. So for instance, although the complex and sensitive issues to do with mercy-killing and euthanasia are beyond the scope of this book, it is worth making the point that killing remains killing even if we attach the word mercy to it.

There are also cases where the word mercy is used to disguise other motives. Imagine, for instance, a situation in which you are working in an organisation and you feel that a colleague is making wrong decisions. So you go to your line manager and raise the matter. He or she agrees with you but refuses to challenge your colleague. When asked why, they reply, 'I want to be merciful.' It sounds good but the reality may well be that the real motive is not in fact mercy but a desire to avoid a confrontation. We need to be merciful but that mercy must be tempered by careful analysis and a scrupulous consideration of what is right and wrong.

Many people in companies or authorities have agreed rules regarding their working practices. We have to be careful that the pursuit of mercy does not encourage us to be dishonest or disloyal to employers. If we have been entrusted with the effective management of a workshop, then it is surely wrong to refuse, on the grounds of mercy, to take disciplinary action against someone who is producing inferior work. Of course, I have to add the caution that if the organisation we work for is immoral or demands that we do things that are wrong, then they have forfeited any right to expect our allegiance. Followers of Jesus will always strive to be faithful servants of their employers but our ultimate commitment is to the King of kings.

On a more domestic scale it is possible, as most parents know, to be too merciful to children. Some sort of discipline must be imposed and here again the competing demands of justice and mercy must be balanced.

Spread the net

We must not define 'mercy' too narrowly, as we have already suggested. It is sadly possible to imagine those who effectively restrict their mercy to one night a week when they go out and give food and blankets to 'down and outs' on the street. For these people it may actually be a real challenge to be merciful at home or at work. For other people it may be a challenge to *extend* their acts of mercy beyond their own situation to the many people in the world who are in desperate need of food, drink, shelter and money. If you are not already involved in very practical acts of mercy I commend to you organisations such as Tearfund and Compassion, who have worked effectively with the world's poor for many decades.

We also need to ensure that we extend our mercy to our own personal relationships. Are you sufficiently kind to your colleagues, family and acquaintances? Do you listen supportively and behave in a caring way? Do you visit them or phone them when they need you? Are you always available for the people who are part of the very fabric of your life? Can you be relied upon to keep confidences or to offer support? Beyond these questions, you also need to ask yourself if you are merciful in terms of both your words and actions. Do you work in a 'bitchy' environment? In your own situation could mercy possibly involve leaving the staff room or canteen when a conversation starts to get vitriolic? Or could it involve speaking up for people who are being unfairly criticised and marginalised? When a person is being condemned in the media it may also be merciful and right (even though it's unpopular) to speak up and remind people to wait for the normal judicial processes to run their course, instead of listening while other people perhaps wrongly condemn someone who is, in fact, 'innocent until proven guilty'. Our first reaction should always be to be merciful.

Finally, we should cast our net wide by praying for people so as to implement a kind of spiritual mercy. If we believe in the power of prayer then the greatest good we can do for someone is to pray for them – but do we? We should always pray regularly and sincerely for the welfare of others.

Let your mercy be costly!

Needless to say, some of our acts of mercy need to involve money. One way in which you might be dealing with this aspect of things is to do what many Christians do and give 10 per cent of your income to charity. (Many give more, of course.)

Some of our acts of mercy need to go beyond the financial, but cost us in other respects. We need to go beyond the clichés of the hard world around us, where people generally 'keep ahead of the pack' by covering their own back, crushing the opposition, firing the failing, teaching competitors a lesson they won't forget, and being the winner who takes all. Instead of treading this path, we need to be merciful by showing kindness, tolerance and decency. When it does come to a fight (either literally or verbally) we say quietly: 'If that's the only way I'm going to win, then I'm not going to try.' It means taking off our armour in life and expecting a few wounds – so the cost is going to be real, even if it isn't financial.

Stay tuned in

A reliable way of reminding ourselves of the nature of mercy on an ongoing basis is to think of mercy in terms of the Trinity, i.e. as something that flows from the Father, the Son, and the Holy Spirit.

First of all, our mercy to others should flow out from our experience of God the Father and His great kindness towards us. We have seen how in the Old Testament mercy is one of God's defining characteristics. Theologians have seen in God the Father the one who loved us so much that He prepared the entire plan through which we might be brought back to Him.

Second, our mercy should be modelled on Jesus, who showed mercy by getting involved with the world, and suffering for the sake of those He loved. I find this a helpful thought because we often see mercy as a quick fix — we dip into our wallet or hastily sign a cheque and that's that. However, viewing mercy as a way of life, day in and day out, reminds us that it may well demand much more. If we think of how Jesus exercised mercy we cannot help but remember the personal cost involved, throughout His life, to the very moment of His death. Clearly, His approach was neither quick nor easy.

Finally, considering mercy in terms of the Holy Spirit will remind us that God can make the impossible possible — because God still acts today through people, by His Holy Spirit. Having God's Spirit dwelling in us can be especially useful in cases where we are confronted with a person whom we do not find it easy to like! This is because mercy is not primarily an action of the emotions, but an expression of the will to be merciful in God's name, knowing that God will help us through the power of the Holy Spirit. It is no bad prayer to come before God and say: 'Lord, I want to show mercy. Please help me to do so through the power of your Holy Spirit.' With or without this prayer, the Holy Spirit will help us to make any act of mercy warm and loving. This is right because mercy should never be the result of following a cold, abstract rule, but the consequence of a living relationship with God, through the bond with His Spirit. Without the power of God's Spirit, our mercy will either dry up or become a façade. We will crack under the strain of trying to manufacture mercy ourselves. God is ready and waiting to give us the strength of His Sprit to give mercy to all – even our toughest enemies.

TO SUM UP

Clearly, if we are to walk on the path of blessing that we trust will lead us to find happiness, we must seek to engage in mercy. After all, how can we be filled with God's Holy Spirit, and at the same time fail to respond to the needs of people around us?

As we have seen, mercy covers a great range of good things. We may think of mercy as being like a mighty, snow-capped mountain range dominating the landscape. While the gentle foothills of kindness and decency are easy to ascend, the higher levels behind them, which involve an encounter with rugged, precipitous faces of tolerance, patience and sympathy, will inevitably be a struggle to climb. Yet behind all these, there are still greater challenges – towering far up into the clouds are the daunting heights of sacrificial love and utter forgiveness which no man or woman can ascend without pain and enormous personal cost. Whether or not we are personally called to scale these heights, we can surely all begin on the ascent, making sure that mercy is not simply an intellectual truth but something that we work out in our lives.

Whatever difficulties we encounter on our path through life, carrying out acts of mercy will certainly bring a reward both in our earthly life and in life after death. This is simply because a merciless approach to life involves acts which erase our humanity and make us dry up deep inside, while a merciful approach fills us with love and compassion, which will give us a whole new experience of the world around us. As we see people affected by our own demonstrations of mercy we will fill full to the brim with a deep happiness that knows we are sharing God's love.

6

Be Pure in Heart!

Blessed are the pure in heart,
for they will see God.
(Matthew 5:8)

PURE NONSENSE?

I suspect readers of this chapter fall into various categories. Some won't have the slightest idea what I'm about to talk about. Others will probably assume I'm going to spend the entire chapter talking about that supposed preoccupation of religious people: sex. I imagine I'm going to teach the first group and surprise the second. Sex will make an appearance, but only briefly.

This particular beatitude doesn't initially seem to have anything to do with happiness. The word 'pure' has a rather limited usage today. We use it with reference to bottled water and to air, as well as in sentences such as, 'It was just pure stupidity!' So is this chapter just going to be filled with nonsense – pure or otherwise? Or is it, like the other beatitudes, going to give us a clue about the path to true happiness?

PURITY DEFINED

The Greek word used here is *katharos* and it has two main senses, each of which has something relevant to say to us about the meaning of purity. The first meaning centres on the idea of being 'clean'. Purity in this sense refers to something not being dirty as in 'clean clothes' or 'lacking contamination'. This meaning is easy to relate to, because we're increasingly aware of contaminants and pollutants nowadays and we all want pure air, pure foods and pure water. The second meaning has a slightly different focus. It implies that something is undivided and has integrity. Our English word also embraces this meaning since someone might say, when asked whether they used their car in London, 'No, *purely* public transport.' The beatitude encompasses both aspects of purity. It refers to the need to have a clean centre to our lives, and a clear focus. As we'll see, it's about having God, His example and His teachings at the very centre of our lives.

GETTING TO THE HEART OF THE MATTER

We also need to consider how Jesus used the word 'heart'. These days we tend to think of the heart primarily as that vital biological pump that keeps the blood flowing and us alive. However, even today, in our age of technology and psychology we still use the word 'heart' to describe that tangled cluster of emotions, drives, demands and motivations that define us individually. During Jesus' day people had no idea about blood circulation but they would certainly have been aware of the thudding organ in their chest and of its crucial importance. They must have known that it had to keep beating and that when it stopped, a person died. They would probably also have realised that excitement or fear makes it beat more quickly. In other words, they too would probably have thought of it as being not just a vital organ, but also an organ that is affected by feelings and thoughts. Given this, we can probably safely assume that our own understanding of the word 'heart' is not so terribly far from the understanding someone would have had when listening to Jesus preach the Sermon on the Mount.

When Jesus referred to the 'heart' He was no doubt referring to the heart of our being, which motivates our actions, manners and words. The heart refers to our inner nature, thoughts and feelings. He was probably looking at what we might call 'internal purity', which relates to the happenings of our hidden (private) inner being. The Beatitudes all focus beyond the superficial, to the depths of the human soul, but this one does so more than others. The reason, as we shall see, is simple. It is all too easy to ignore internal purity and instead create a faith that revolves around external actions and preparations.

WHY FOCUS ON INTERNAL PURITY?

The main reason is that we're all likely to focus on external delusions, surface appearance or image rather than on internal realities. Although we may not be remotely inclined to respond in the judgemental way the Pharisees did in Jesus' time, we are all still at risk of aiming for *external* purity.

In Jesus' day the word 'pure' immediately made people think of things they should or shouldn't do. This is clear when you consider how many tomes were written on how to interpret the Ten Commandments in day-to-day life (as we shall see shortly). Because the concept is so foreign to us in our contemporary society we need to continue to explore it carefully.

When we think about concepts of purity and contamination in the modern West, we tend to think in terms of hygiene and the transmission of disease. Hence, when we meet observant Jews, Muslims and other groups who believe they must avoid touching or eating certain things, and who engage in ritual washings, we assume that this is something similar to our own hygiene rules.

In fact, this sort of religious action has almost nothing to do with protection from dirt or bacteria. Its significance revolves around being clean from spiritual contamination.

For a Jew in Jesus' day there was a whole number of things that could contaminate or defile you. Many of these things had been explained in the Old Testament books of Leviticus and Deuteronomy. By Jesus' time, the rules had been endlessly multiplied and elaborated by generations of religious leaders. You could be rendered ritually impure by such things as making contact with a dead body, touching certain animals (most famously, pigs), having certain skin diseases, and – if you were a woman – by giving birth to a child or menstruating. This contamination was serious. It meant that you could not take part in temple worship, and in some cases you had to keep yourself temporarily separate from your friends and relatives. In some circumstances people had to be 'purified' by under-going special washing rituals. In fact, there was an extraordi-nary emphasis on external purity and archaeologists have commented on the vast numbers of ritual bathing spots and cisterns found in Israel.

Issues relating to ritual purity even underlie the crucifixion. For a Jew the real horror of the cross was probably not the pain but the fact that it was such a cursed death (see Deuteronomy 21:23 and Galatians 3:13), through which victims became unclean beyond any hope of redemption. People cared passionately about these external aspects of purity because they thought ritual purity would enable them to enter into a right relationship with God. The issue of what we might call being focused on externals or religious ritualism centred around the Pharisees, a group within the Jewish faith, who specialised in defining the rules on what *exactly* was ritually clean and unclean. Notoriously, they not only defined the rules but went about (with the interfering self-righteousness common to such people) making sure that everybody kept such rules. To use a phrase by Mark Twain, they were 'good men in the worst sense of the word'.

It is worth saying that, at this time, the Jewish faith was doubly threatened: on the one hand by the brutal Roman rule and on the other by the more subtle threat of the spreading and very pagan Greek culture. An emphasis on external purity acted as a preservative for Jewish culture. Unfortunately, preservatives can be pretty toxic, and this was.

But having a faith dominated by 'externals', which is what we might call a spiritual life centring on rules, regulations and actions, isn't something that died out with the Pharisees. It is alive and well and, for many people, *is* religion. In fact, even in Christianity, which ought to be immune to it, the idea that faith is to be dominated by externals sprouts up regularly, like some persistent weed.

It's unlikely that you're guilty of this kind of superficial religion. However, let's consider it for a moment because it's surprisingly easy to get drawn into this trap. For example, someone who goes along to church (or the mosque or synagogue) *only* because it's expected of them by their society, their community, their family or their partner is engaging in what I would call 'fake religion'. There's a lot of this today, but this is not a new phenomenon. A hundred years ago it might have been a question of attending church because your boss was a churchwarden or an elder and it didn't hurt your promotion prospects. Today, we get people attending church to get their children into the local school, which has church affiliations. There are also people who enthusiastically send their children to Sunday school just so that they can get some peace and quiet on a Sunday morning.

Increasingly too, we hear of people through opinion polls who identify themselves as Christian even though they don't believe in Christ. In many cases they tick the 'Christian' box because they want to be considered culturally 'Christian', rather than being of another religion. I presume that all such people are under no illusion that they are religious and that they realise that they are, in effect, merely camouflaged agnostics.

In this beatitude Jesus is addressing the 'shallow-faith community'. In other words, He's addressing people who see themselves as religious but who, in reality, merely have an inadequate and superficial faith based on external actions alone. Most people who are guilty of having a 'shallow faith' are not at all inclined to see their faith as being in any way shallow or inadequate. After all, everybody can see the many good and visible things they do in the name of their faith.

THE DANGER OF HAVING A FAITH FOCUSED ON 'EXTERNALS'

Let's summarise a few of the problems surrounding religion based solely on external actions. But before we do, I want to say that, criticisms notwithstanding, I am often greatly impressed and often humbled by the discipline and dedication shown by those whose lives are ruled by such externals as ritual purity, fasting, giving sacrifices and making pilgrimages.

Life becomes too complicated

To seek purity through doing or avoiding external things is to have your life governed by rules. Very well, but what exactly are the rules? How *precisely* are they to be kept? In order to avoid what might seem to be criticism of any existing religion let me make up an imaginary one: let's call it Supafaith. (I'm pretty sure it doesn't exist but if it does, my apologies to its adherents.) In our hypothetical Supafaith, let's imagine that believers must bow north three times at the start of the day. Straightforward, surely? But what happens when you don't know what direction north is?

What happens if, for medical reasons, you are unable to bow? How many degrees out are you allowed to be? Is that magnetic north or grid north? What happens to Supafaith explorers at the South Pole where every direction is north or at the North Pole where every direction is south? Oh, and what about Supafaith astronauts? In addition, imagine that Supafaith has strict dietary requirements, which include the rule that its followers must not eat lemons. Surely that's easy? Yes, but does that include lemonade? Or lemon cake? What about synthetic lemon flavouring? What about fruits related to lemons, such as limes? What about a slice of lemon in a drink? What about lemon-scented washing-up liquid?

Do you see how it all spirals out of control? Very soon you end up needing some sort of specialised religious court to issue rulings on the least detail of existence and post a constantly evolving checklist of what must (and must not) be done, eaten, drunk or touched. And of course there must always be that lingering doubt: did you really perform all the rituals properly? Can you be absolutely certain you were not accidentally in contact with something that renders you unclean? The result is that life becomes a traumatic, draining and never-ending walk through a minefield of obstacles.

It leads to a misplaced focus

Another very serious criticism of religious ritualism is that it encourages us to misplace our faith. Let's agree that the basis of faith is Almighty God and our relationship with Him. Yet in a life dominated by religious rituals, God Himself can somehow get pushed out. We become so busy attending services, saying the right things and doing the right things (and avoiding the wrong ones) that our relationship with God takes a back seat. You've probably been present at one of those amusing occasions where an infant has been given a wrapped-up present only to ignore it, becoming happily preoccupied with the wrapping paper. Religious ritualism is like that, only it isn't amusing. In trying to seek external purity people become obsessed with the trappings of religion rather than the vital living relationship that should be at its core. In its most developed form, religious ritualism can actually be a bizarre form of idolatry, a thing that takes the place of God.

It leads to an inconsistent life

A subtle danger of religious ritualism is that it can lead to a growing discrepancy between external appearance and internal reality. We can acquire a gleaming façade of decency while, underneath the gloss, a foul rottenness develops. We may become a real *hypocrite*, a word which in the original Greek meant an actor in a play and the mask they wore. Hypocrisy is a perilous condition not because it fools God or our friends and neighbours (which it doesn't), but because it may well fool us personally. In other words, we may feel we are spiritually well when, in fact, we're in urgent need of help.

Here, once more, we find ourselves addressing the matter of happiness. Whatever your views, you must agree that to be in a situation where there is a major mismatch between your internal wishes and your external actions is a recipe for unhappiness at best and, at worst, full psychological breakdown. Having this lack of integrity is disastrous, which we are reminded of if we note that the negative of 'integrity' is related linguistically to the word 'disintegration'.

You are probably familiar with the phrase 'Jekyll and Hyde'. It comes from a story by the Victorian writer Robert Louis Stevenson which centres on an odd and apparently inexplicable link between two characters: Henry Jekyll, a thoroughly respectable doctor, and Edward Hyde, a violent and evil man. It eventually transpires that these two people are in fact one and the same person. Jekyll has taken a potion that turns him into Hyde. Eventually the Hyde character takes over and destroys Jekyll. The tale is a profound illustration that a pleasant exterior may mask a grotesque interior. More disturbingly, it warns us that in the end, a shallow crust of goodness may not be enough to restrain an active core of evil.

It's far too superficial

If we are preoccupied with seeking external purity there is a very real danger that we will create a godless vacuum at the core of our lives. Imagine if you went to the doctor feeling desperately ill and all he or she did was ask a few basic questions, stare at you and mutter, 'Well, you look all right to me.' We wouldn't be happy with this kind of superficial treatment. We would (rightly) expect our pulse to be taken, chest to be listened to, blood samples and X-rays to be taken and, possibly, for some invasive exploratory tests to be ordered. We know that a visual examination is inadequate simply because – as is widely recognised – external appearances can be deceptive.

In a religion preoccupied with externals, people examine how they're doing by looking at external matters such as what you touch (or don't), what you eat (or don't), what you say (or don't) and how you worship. If you pass these tests, you consider yourself to be fine. So a modern person might say, 'I got through today without swearing and without looking at dodgy websites, and I even attend church on Sunday, so I'm okay.' At the same time, he or she harboured bitter and angry thoughts all day, which might later lead to actions far out of alignment from God's will. In other words, the superficial religious actions might effectively be 'papering over the cracks in life' and those same 'cracks' might eventually lead to all kinds of sin.

It's easy to see how closely actions are related to thoughts if we consider any violent incident. It's often possible to trace its roots to anger. In the case of a theft, it's probably possible to trace the action back to greed or covetousness, and in the case of a rape, we could probably trace the action back to lustful thoughts or unresolved past sexual abuse. In other words, the thought is the father of the deed.

When people's lives are dominated by religious ritualism, it's all too easy to dismiss thoughts as being unimportant. However, these very thoughts ferment and bubble away with an ever-growing intensity and eventually provoke us to action. When they've fermented for a while it's then too late for all the constraints of religious rules to stop them doing any harm. It has been wisely said that the heart of the problem of the human race is the problem of the human heart. What we do on the outside doesn't actually solve what goes on inside. Faith preoccupied with externals offers us a plaster, when what we actually need is surgery.

'Externals' can too easily dominate

Even modern Christians can be guilty of losing their focus on internal purity because of a focus on externals. Although, in theory, Christianity has almost no rituals (what we call 'Communion' and baptism being the exceptions) and although Christianity has never legislated on how we should live, Christians of almost every tradition have managed to shift the focus of faith to externals and this has stopped them from focusing on developing inner purity. This has happened in various ways to all denominations, including the Protestant branch of Christianity to which I belong. What is good and right is accentuated and a list of rules dominates what it is to be a Christian. Religious rules often take the place of relationship with Christ.

In one church group, for example, 'right behaviour' has replaced a real experience of Christ. Not missing church services, not buying raffle tickets, skipping certain (or all) films and not using swear words have become hallmarks of 'the good Christian'. What were once merely good practices and wise actions became rigid rules that clearly mark out the 'faithful' from the 'lax' or 'back-slidden' believer. Any necessity to develop internal purity has been utterly obscured by these rules.

In another group, 'social involvement' has become the main emphasis. The pressing needs of the world have become so dominant that the faith now revolves almost entirely around such things as helping the poor, facilitating economic development, fighting injustice, campaigning about global warming, and so on. Of course, these are important issues, and we will return to how we are to approach them later, but do you see the problem? People are distracted from the necessity to develop internal purity, this time not so much by external rules as by external priorities. The result is the same. The priority of personally dealing with God has been pushed to one side. The vital necessity of internal godliness has been totally obscured by a preoccupation with *external* godliness.

In another case, it is an obsession with religious rules and beliefs that takes people away from a focus on inner purity. The goal of sticking to 'sound beliefs' dominates people's daily thoughts. The preservation of truth and the careful defining and exposing of wrong beliefs has come to dominate these people's religion. Sermons become warnings against heresy or a damning indictment of the doctrinal weaknesses of other churches or denominations. Any emphasis on having a genuine and lively relationship with God, of being pure in heart, has somehow been forgotten.

If you are a Christian, can I plead with you that whatever church you are in, you take Jesus' words seriously? Make it your priority to develop purity of heart – i.e. to get and remain right with God. Make that the foundation stone of your life and the rest of the Christian faith will fall into place. Get it wrong and everything else, however good, will fall apart. The sad fact is that we are all tempted to let the focus of our religion slip away from internal purity to external matters. This is because it's quite simply much easier to deal with godliness and good behaviour than it is to deal with God Himself.

JESUS' OWN VIEW

When God-incarnate walked on this earth, His view of these risks was very clear. Jesus repeatedly challenged people when they focused on externals alone or when their faith was merely superficial. This in itself gave rise to controversy.

For example, in Matthew 15 we read that Jesus was asked why His disciples didn't ritually wash their hands before meals according 'to the tradition of the elders'. His response was first to denounce any religious observance in which tradition overrode the word of God. He then taught that cleanliness was a matter of what came out of the mouth not what went into it. 'Don't you see that whatever enters the mouth goes into the stomach and then out of the body?' He explained. 'But the things that come out of the mouth come from the heart, and these make a man "unclean". For out of the heart come evil thoughts, murder, adultery, sexual immorality, theft, false testimony, slander. These are what make a man "unclean"; but eating with unwashed hands does not make him "unclean"' (Matthew 15:17–20).

At other times Jesus repeatedly and quite deliberately disregarded many of the taboos of the Jewish faith. He touched lepers and dead bodies and let Himself be touched by a woman whose gynaecological problem left her permanently 'unclean' (Luke 5:12–15; Mark 5:39–40). He had dealings with people who were ritually and spiritually unclean, such as tax collectors who were in regular contact with the 'contaminated' Gentiles. Jesus also broke the laws on what it was permissible to do on the Sabbath (Matthew 12:1–14; Mark 2:23 – 3:6; Luke 13:10–17; 14:1–6).

While openly criticising a shallow, ritualistic approach to faith, Jesus emphasised the necessity for a faith focused on internal transformation, which is only possible when a person has a deep relationship with God. The following words, from Luke's Gospel, are typical of His attitude:

> No good tree bears bad fruit, nor does a bad tree bear good fruit. Each tree is recognised by its own fruit. People do not pick figs from thorn bushes, or grapes from briers. The good man brings good things out of the good stored up in his heart, and the evil man brings evil things out of the evil stored up in his heart. For out of the overflow of his heart his mouth speaks. (Luke 6:43–45)

Jesus' logic here is worth carefully considering. First of all, He says, it is the heart that is ultimately responsible for our actions. The equation He makes is a simple one: a pure heart produces good actions, while an impure heart produces bad actions. Secondly, the link from heart to actions is a one-way street. In other words, while a good heart will produce good deeds, good deeds will not produce a good heart.

The central focus of Jesus' teaching was the coming of the kingdom of God and this has a considerable bearing on this matter of a religion based on externals. We tend to misunderstand the concept of the kingdom of God and think of it as a geographical region. It's an easy mistake to make, especially since some of us live in what is rather optimistically called the 'United Kingdom'. What Jesus was referring to was a world in which God rules as king. The Bible makes it clear that getting into the kingdom involves accepting a personal relationship with God in which we accept His authority. The principle of having a right relationship with God is therefore at the very heart of the idea of the kingdom of God.

Because Jesus dismissed the idea of finding salvation through external purity, some people see Him as a radical innovator. Although He was certainly an innovator, ushering in new, life-changing teachings of God, much of His teaching on purity simply cleared away the distortions that had come to obscure the true faith of the Old Testament. Any careful reading of the Old Testament will show many places where the prophets condemned shallow, empty, ritual religion and encouraged a living, heart-centred faith. Consider the following passages from the Psalms:

> Who may ascend the hill of the LORD?
>   Who may stand in his holy place?
> He who has clean hands and a pure heart,
>   who does not lift up his soul to an idol
>   or swear by what is false.
> He will receive blessing from the LORD
>   and vindication from God his Saviour.
> Such is the generation of those who seek him,
>   who seek your face, O God of Jacob.
> (Psalm 24:3–6)

> Create in me a pure heart, O God,
>   and renew a steadfast spirit within me.
> Do not cast me from your presence
>   or take your Holy Spirit from me.
> Restore to me the joy of your salvation
>   and grant me a willing spirit, to sustain me.
> (Psalm 51:10–12)

The writer of Proverbs counselled: 'above all else, guard your heart, for it is the wellspring of life' (Proverbs 4:23). In another famous verse we read that 'people judge by outward appearance, but the

LORD looks at the heart' (1 Samuel 16:7, NLT). The reality is that, in advocating what we might call 'heart religion' over dead rituals, Jesus was following many of the Old Testament prophets, such as Amos, Isaiah and Jeremiah (as evidenced in Amos 5:21–26; Isaiah 1:10–17; and Jeremiah 7:21–24).

Despite this, it would be a mistake to see Jesus as no more than simply another great prophet of revival in the long Jewish tradition. He certainly did make a radical break with many of the rules of the Judaism of His day, for example dismissing the well-established dietary laws (Mark 7:1–23). Doing this alone was so radical that it was only after some considerable hesitation (and divine prodding) that the early church followed His lead (Acts 10:1 – 11:18).

We see further evidence that Jesus downplayed religion based on externals through the simple fact that Christianity throughout its history has disregarded a focus on purity through external rituals – involving things such as what is eaten, drunk or touched. Among the three faiths which can be traced back to Abraham (Judaism, Christianity and Islam – sometimes known as 'Abrahamic faiths') Christianity is unique in this respect. The apostle Paul wholeheartedly rejected external demonstrations of supposed purity in Colossians 2:20–23, no doubt because of Jesus' teaching, and although churches since then have certainly added rules and regulations these have always appeared to be later creations. The only satisfactory explanation for this odd status of Christianity is the one presented by the New Testament itself: Jesus effectively ordered His followers *to prioritise the business of getting their hearts right with God.* Jesus does not abolish the laws but looks to the heart of the matter. Jesus said, not only should we not commit adultery, we should not have lust in our hearts. Later in the Sermon on the Mount He said: 'You have heard that it was said to the people long ago, "Do not murder, and anyone who murders will be subject to judgment"' (Matthew 5:21).

So Jesus is concerned with externals *and* He takes matters deeper to look at what is in the heart.

THE PATH TO TRUE PURITY

Having looked at what we should *avoid*, we now need to consider how we can go about becoming pure in heart. In Matthew's Gospel Jesus is recorded as having said: 'Love the Lord your God with all your heart and with all your soul and with all your mind. This is the first and greatest commandment' (Matthew 22:37). This is very clearly our main means to purity. Doing this means having no divided loyalties and it also means being fully focused on God. It means enthroning God in our lives and proclaiming His character in all we are and do. It means putting Him in charge in every possible area of our lives. To put it snappily, it means being 'pure to the core' (as opposed to 'rotten to the core'). If this seems a tall order, then at least remember that the core of Christianity is forgiveness for our failings! Immediately following Jesus' Sermon on the Mount where He gave the Beatitudes and set the highest moral standards, Jesus taught His disciples how to pray. Central to this prayer is that we can come to God, our Father, and ask for forgiveness. Jesus knows that all humans fall short of the perfect standards set by God and reminds us that we can run to our heavenly Father and ask forgiveness.

It's important to remember this gospel of forgiveness because we have to acknowledge that generations of Christians have found that while it is easy to declare Christ as Lord it is a true challenge to live this out. On a purely practical level, then, we need to consider how we can aim for this purity of heart. Here are a few suggestions, all of which are intended to be as practical as possible.

Examine your heart

Our first and most essential step must be to examine ourselves, remembering that we can sin 'in thought, word and deed'.

Thoughts

Considering our thoughts first, we need to ask ourselves what our minds dwell on daily. What preoccupies us or even obsesses us? What in our thinking is the 'centre of gravity' around which everything in our lives rotates? Is it our job, our family, our figure, the food we eat, our bank balance or the pleasures we experience or long for? Although none of these things are evil in themselves, they can certainly take us away from purity if they become the focus of our attention. If we allow our whole lives to revolve around any one of them we become imbalanced and less pure. In the same vein, we need to ask ourselves if God is at the centre of our thinking or if He is at the periphery or even largely absent? Do the sinful emotions of greed, pride, lust, anger and disobedience run unchecked through our lives? Is it possible that you yourself have created a shining façade of religiousness to cover up an underlying misplaced focus? Do you find yourself feeling contempt for people beneath you in the hierarchy or do you envy people above you? If your thought-life were suddenly projected onto a big screen would you be embarrassed by what other people would see? Someone wisely said, 'Blessed are the pure in heart, for they have nothing to hide,' because one of the defining features of purity of heart is a willingness to be utterly transparent. We also have to 'own' our thoughts and not try to deny that we have them. We must be honest before God who is unshockable.

Words

Returning to examining our thoughts, words and deeds, we must next consider what we say. Are our words fair, decent and honest? Are our words a blessing or a curse to other people? Is there a hurtful edge to anything we say? Is that sharpness that we think of as our 'stimulating wit' experienced very differently by other people? If our words were recorded (which, in fact, they are – since God sees and hears everything) would they constitute evidence against us? In a little letter towards the end of the New Testament, James, a leader of the early church, talks a lot about how we misuse language. He is particularly hard on people who one minute talk piously and the next become abusive (James 3:1–12). Consistency here, as elsewhere, is a major virtue. So we need to ask ourselves if we praise self-sacrifice and humility on Sundays, and then merrily spend the rest of the week boosting our ego.

Deeds

Finally, we need to consider our actions. What are you doing with your life? How do you spend your time? What do you do when you have a few minutes free? Are you generous with your resources of finances, time, talents and energy? In this respect it's good to remember that although most of us are in the habit of talking about '*my* time' and '*my* money', they're not actually ours. In reality, we don't own a thing. Everything we have is merely on loan to us from God for a relatively short period while on earth. One day we'll each be asked to account for how we've used or abused whatever we've been entrusted with. Then, retrospectively, we'll need to answer the question: 'How did you behave in your life?'

When we examine ourselves in terms of each of these three areas, we need to make sure we turn on a floodlight that illuminates everything, rather than a tightly focused spotlight that highlights only specific areas. It's all too easy to decide to be ruthless only about sins we're not especially prone to. The most obvious case is those elderly church ministers who have forgotten what hormones feel like, thundering from the pulpit against 'the desires of youth', yet in their own lives they use their finances for flagrant material pleasure. And there are many similar but subtler tricks. People who are affluent tend to come down heavily on the sins of the less well-off – for example, on their restlessness and envy. Those who are impoverished tend to return the favour by being critical of the pride and complacency of the rich. The comfortably married criticise the longing of singles for relationships and those who are single criticise the married for their 'idolatry of the family'.

In other words, we need to remember when we're examining ourselves that it's always so much easier to see the sins of others and to turn a blind eye to our own faults. Jesus addressed this issue of judging others. He said:

> Do not judge, or you too will be judged. For in the same way you judge others, you will be judged, and with the measure you use, it will be measured to you. Why do you look at the speck of sawdust in your brother's eye and pay no attention to the plank in your own eye? How can you say to your brother, 'Let me take the speck out of your eye,' when all the time there is a plank in your own eye? You hypocrite, first take the plank out of your own eye, and then you will see clearly to remove the speck from your brother's eye. (Matthew 7:1–5)

Practically, Christians have always found it a great help to carefully and prayerfully read God's word, the Bible, asking for God's Holy Spirit to point out those things that offend Him. If you do that, it is very striking how frequently passages or stories in the Bible can suddenly come alive and, as it were, point the finger to our own weaknesses and deficiencies. The Psalmist provides a wonderful prayer to ask God, 'Search me, O God, and know my heart; test me and know my anxious thoughts. See if there is any offensive way in me, and lead me in the way everlasting' (Psalm 139:23–24).

When thinking about our deeds, we also need to avoid focusing only on the spectacular sins. Yes, of course, hatred, bitterness and lust are bad and we need to try and do something about them; but there are many other sins. If you talk about health risks to people who have worked in jungles, you will often hear them say that it is not spectacular things such as the snakes, tigers or crocodiles that pose the deadly perils, but the invisible bacteria and viruses. So it is in the jungles of our hearts; what may be fatal to us is something that we might not even consider to be a problem. What we tell ourselves is our 'commendable ambition' may in fact be a ruthless trampling over others in order to gratify our own ego. Desire to provide 'a decent standard of living for the family' may, if we are honest, actually be naked greed. We are particularly good at disguising sins and it may even be that what we see as a virtue is actually a vice. Sometimes it is the subtle sins, rather than the spectacular ones, that ultimately cripple us.

Accept forgiveness

It's extremely challenging examining our minds, speech and actions, but it needn't be a negative process. We are often hesitant in admitting our sins to God because we are afraid He will not love us or forgive us. When the first humans Adam and Eve sinned, they hid from God (Genesis 3). Yet God called out to them and immediately desired to talk with them. From the moment humanity turned against God, He continually reached out to rescue His people. When we feel afraid to approach God with our shortcomings, we must remind ourselves of the character of God. God is just and merciful. The Psalmist said it perfectly: 'The LORD is compassionate and gracious, slow to anger, abounding in love. He will not always accuse, nor will he harbour his anger for ever; he does not treat us as our sins deserve or repay us according to our iniquities' (Psalm 103:8–10). We must remember that there is not one thing we have done that God is not ready and waiting to forgive. Like a loving Father, God is waiting for us to come to Him. Jesus said that God is like a shepherd who runs after the lost sheep. Throughout history, God has constantly called out to people to come to Him to be cleansed and forgiven.

If you accept God's forgiveness for what you've thought, said or done wrong, this whole process of re-evaluation can be extremely constructive and can lead to a healthy refocusing and redirecting of energies. Putting your faith in Jesus really does make you part of God's family. You become, in a real sense, one of Jesus Christ's brothers or sisters and you have God as your loving, heavenly parent.

This very fact should give you an utterly unshakeable and secure basis for self-examination because you should understand that anything undesirable you see in yourself will not be judged or used as a reason to write you off. Your own acknowledgement of failings can lead to a recognition of God's enormous love, which extended to dying a horrible and humiliating death on a cross, just so that you could be brought back into that divine family. As it says in 1 John 1:7, 'the blood of Jesus, his Son, cleanses us from all sin' (NLT).

The greater the unpleasantness you find within, the more firmly you grasp onto God's mercy and love. Being – or becoming – a Christian will give you a really strong foundation to stand on. If probing around inside to see what makes you tick ends up with you running in despair to God to seek His mercy and forgiveness, you are a blessed person!

Even if you find your motives are relatively pure already, seeking purity of heart will always bring us back to our need for forgiveness. After all, we are all, unfortunately, far from perfect!

Accepting God's forgiveness in this way quite simply means acting on what you find. Suppose you bought an old house only to realise, when investigating the cellars, that the floor beams looked dodgy. How would you feel if you called in an expert and he or she just poked, tut-tutted and then considered at great length which particular type of dry rot you had? You might well say: 'I don't care what type it is! I just want to know how we can fix it.' In the same way, self-examination becomes nonsensical if we only draw up neat categories of failings. We can, on the other hand, make it a valuable process if we bring our weakness to God and ask Him to strengthen or correct it. Ask for forgiveness through the blood of Jesus Christ, plead for the power of the Holy Spirit to help you overcome your sin and then accept the forgiveness that is offered to you. If you do that, you'll be in a perfect position to move forward victoriously in life. With all confidence we can wake every day knowing we are loved unconditionally and forgiven completely.

A few key points to remember:

God is *always* quick and ready to forgive if we are repentant.

There is not one thing we do that God is not ready to forgive. No matter how offensive, grievous, callous or heinous your sin, God deeply longs to forgive you and set you free.

Once you have repented and asked for forgiveness, know you have been forgiven. *Do not* take it back. We must receive the forgiveness God has given us. When we meditate on our sins and see ourselves as worthless, it is like looking at the cross and saying, 'Your sacrifice, Jesus, was not good enough for me to be forgiven.' God longs for us to receive forgiveness and then not take it back. Receive the forgiveness that comes through Christ!

Keep on cleaning!

Whenever you clean or purify something, whether it's your kitchen or anything else, it's always worthwhile resolving to keep it clean in the future and not let the dirt build up again. This applies to keeping the core of our lives pure. We have to remember that becoming pure in heart will involve repeated clean-ups throughout our lives.

This has always been something of a problem for Christians. After all, we believe in a once-and-for-all point of conversion because you only 'become' a Christian once, through a process which has come to be known as being 'born again'. (This is referred to specifically in John 3:3, 7, where the need for this one-off event is emphasised so that we can be adopted into the family of God.) However, we must remember that this initial rebirth is just the beginning of a long period of growth, in the same way as a human physical birth is only the beginning of a long period of growth. Some branches of the Church have talked about Christian morality and overlooked the necessity for conversion and surrender to Jesus. Other branches have talked so much about conversion that they have overlooked the need for moral growth. We need to take a more balanced view, which recognises the need not only for an initial good old clear out, but also ongoing cleaning sessions.

On a purely practical level, here are a few ideas for ongoing cleaning:

Pray regularly

It's a good idea to set aside some time each day specifically to talk to God. When you pray, it's helpful if you do it in a quiet place where other people won't distract you. Talk to God in your own language and be prepared to listen to what he has to say to you. Try not to be led by your own issues and desires, but focus on worship and adoration of God. It's good to start with this, which can lead into a confession of your sins. Then express your thanks for all the good things that God has given you. Finally, you may want to bring some requests to God. Putting worship, confession and thanksgiving first stops our prayer times becoming purely a shopping list of requests.

Read your Bible

In the Psalms we read, 'How can a young man keep his way pure? By living according to your word' (Psalm 119:9), and, 'I have hidden your word in my heart that I might not sin against you' (Psalm 119:11). That ancient advice is very useful in helping us maintain purity of heart. When it comes to Bible reading, get a reliable version that you can understand. For native English speakers, I recommend the NIV (the New International Version), the NLT (the New Living Translation) or the NRSV (the New Revised Standard Version). Many people find a regular Bible-reading programme with explanatory notes helpful; examples include Scripture Union's *Daily Bread* (see www.dailybread.org.uk) or *Explore* produced by the Good Book Company (www.thegoodbook.co.uk; click on 'Bible Reading Notes'). The key point is that you should see the Bible not as a storybook about a fascinating past or as an obscure manuscript to decode, but as a means through which God will speak to you today. Expect His word to say something to you!

Join a church

It's vital to join and regularly attend a church so that you can have fellowship with other believers, receive teaching about the Bible, and receive the sacraments. It's actually a *discipline* to attend church regularly. In a way it's a bit like going to a gym. While you know it's enormously valuable to you, there will be times when you don't enjoy it and other times when you just won't want to bother at all. Persist! The author of the book of Hebrews writes: 'Let us consider how we may spur one another on towards love and good deeds. Let us not give up meeting together, as some are in the habit of doing, but let us encourage one another' (Hebrews 10:24–25).

God has always worked through community. The Old Testament depicts God choosing a people, the Israelites, to be His representatives to the world. The New Testament shows God establishing a new community of faith in Jesus, the church, to be His ambassadors on earth. The Apostle Paul talks about the church as the body of Christ and how each member is vital to God. We are all part of the body and need one another. Paul wrote:

> The eye cannot say to the hand, 'I don't need you!' And the head cannot say to the feet, 'I don't need you!' On the contrary . . . there should be no division in the body, but that its parts have equal concern for each other. If one part suffers, every part suffers with it; if one part is honoured, every part rejoices with it. Now you are the body of Christ and each one of you is a part of it. (1 Corinthians 12:21–27)

The early followers of Jesus knew the power of worshipping together. Luke, the writer of Acts, tells us that the early disciples of Christ,

> . . . devoted themselves to the apostles' teaching and to the fellowship, to the breaking of bread, and to prayer . . . All the believers were together and had everything in common . . . Every day they continued to meet together in the temple courts. They broke bread in their homes and ate together with glad and sincere hearts, praising God and enjoying the favour of all the people. And the Lord added to their number daily those who were being saved. (Acts 2:42–47)

One of the problems we have today, largely due to the availability of the car, is that we have the possibility of attending a large number of different churches. Why is this a problem? The answer is that it is all too easy to seek out somewhere that will comfort us rather than challenge us. A church should never confirm us in our prejudices or encourage us in our complacency; on the contrary, both prejudice and complacency need rebuking. One aspect of church that many people have found to be especially helpful is small study groups (often called cells, pastorates, or home groups), where a small number of people in an informal setting worship, pray and work through a passage of the Bible together. Doing this is very useful, especially because it will give you the opportunity to ask questions about the meaning of a certain passage or (just as importantly) how it applies to your present situation.

Be accountable

It's very useful to find someone whom you trust and respect as a believer in Christ, with whom you can be honest and whom you can have as a companion in the faith. In the best sort of accountability, you and the other person both have the right to ask hard questions. For obvious reasons, this will help your ongoing self-examination and 'cleaning up' process.

Set yourself high targets

It's all too easy to look around us and think that we're better than other people. This is nothing but a recipe for mediocrity. Set the highest possible standards. Aim for the highest heights and when you fall short you will still have achieved something creditable.

Know your own weaknesses

Each of us is prone to different temptations. For example, while some people are tempted to gamble, others don't feel the slightest inclination. While some people are likely to become proud, others just don't have the personality for that. Men and women are also often tempted in very different areas. Given this variation it's obviously wise to know your own weaknesses so you can watch out for them! Whenever you do learn about a particular area in which you know you can't trust yourself, make a mental note to avoid getting yourself into a situation where you'll be tempted, as far as is reasonably possible.

In other words, in these and other ways, recognise that you need to keep on working at purity of heart in order to achieve it. Keep on cleaning!

Have purity of purpose

Alongside the determination you'll need to keep on persevering with the 'cleaning' necessary for the development of purity, you'll also need a good sense of direction. After all, what use is an expensive car with a powerful engine and a focused driver if it's driving along the wrong road? And what use is it if the driver keeps changing his mind about the route?

We need to remember the aspect of the word 'pure' that indicates a focused and integrated completeness. In other words, being pure in heart means more than avoiding sins – it also means knowing what we want and seeking that goal with single-minded determination. It involves having purity of purpose, with no mixed motives.

We read about this in the Old Testament in Psalm 86:11: 'Teach me your way, O LORD, and I will walk in your truth; give me an undivided heart, that I may fear your name.' I like the expression 'an undivided heart'. In the New Testament, in Matthew 6:24, Jesus refers to the same thing: 'No one can serve two masters. Either he will hate the one and love the other, or he will be devoted to the one and despise the other. You cannot serve both God and Money.' I'm sure you, like me, have had the experience when driving along a motorway of suddenly having to make a decision between two or three lanes. Do we stay on the motorway, do we turn off, and if so, do we go west or east? Trying to do all three, or nothing at all, will result in an unpleasant crash. We often face the same kind of decision in life. Dithering or trying to strike a compromise often has catastrophic or at best disappointing results. We must examine our motives.

Think about anyone who has got to the top of his or her profession, whether as a scientist, musician, dancer or athlete. It's almost certain they did not get to that position simply by some accident of birth ('Daddy got me the job') or by drifting into the situation. They will no doubt have got where they are as a result of dedication and persistence. If you know anybody who is a high-level athlete you will know that they spend an extraordinary amount of time honing their muscles and developing their skills. Sometimes they will have done a couple of hours in the gym or swimming pool before you or I even get out of bed!

We also need to remember that it's not simply effort that will have made it possible for people to get to the top; they will also have made major sacrifices. Imagine a top surgeon, for example: they will inevitably have made sacrifices in their social lives. Think of all those weekends when they were on call and unable to go out with friends or family. Consider all those long hours on duty at the hospital and the seemingly endless study for repeated examinations. Their achievement involved countless sacrifices.

In everything, success depends not just on talent but also on dedication and a willingness to accept the cost. The sole exception is the lottery and this very fact explains its attraction. People who reach the top in life see what they want, count the cost and put their goal first. They have purity of purpose. If you talk to anybody at their point of success they will often say things like, 'Well, you know I've been working towards this for twenty-five years.'

Sometimes it's difficult for us to have this purity of purpose because society can pressurise us to drift along and take life as it comes. Going against the flow for whatever reason (and certainly for matters of faith) is rather unusual. It may also be difficult for us to maintain purity of purpose because of the number of things that distract us. Every day, we're bombarded with adverts, media reports or junk mail that try to inspire us to buy this, do that, belong here, go there. The result is that we end up hopelessly multitasking, trying to do several different things at once. This leads to the inevitable result that we never do anything particularly well. Taking this into account, it's easy to see how this beatitude relates to happiness and profound satisfaction, because maintaining purity of purpose is likely to lead to us achieving our objectives. One reason for our discontent is the fact that we strive to do far too much and fail at it. Were we to do a little effectively, we might find ourselves feeling much more content.

When people don't maintain purity of purpose their faith becomes one of many things which needs to be 'slotted in'. As one person observed, since people started inventing labour-saving devices, life has never been busier! With many things vying for our attention, it's all too easy to make the Christian life less than our number one priority. As I look around, I am uncomfortably reminded that many people treat their Christian faith as something rather like a bolt-on accessory to life. For most of the week they are dentists, lawyers, plumbers, homemakers or whatever and *that* is the core of their existence. Then, when it comes to Sunday, they put on their Christianity 'hat', turn up to church and think (or try to think) about God for an hour or so. Then they leave church and the *real* them – the dentist, lawyer or whatever – reasserts itself. This should not be the case. Being pure in heart – pure to the core – means making our faith central to our entire existence. Our faith needs to be so integrated into our lives that it couldn't be separated from everything else.

I often talk to people about how to communicate their faith and sometimes I find that their faith has become so confined to a compartment of their life that they find it extremely difficult to bring it naturally into conversation without it sounding thoroughly artificial. I believe that the good news of Jesus Christ is so serious that it needs to be more than a part-time occupation. It needs to be a permanent preoccupation! If Christianity is true, then nothing else in this world can be more important. It cannot be a supporting act in the drama of our existence or a side menu on the table of life. It absolutely *must* take first place. We must not serve two masters! Having purity of purpose means that God alone must take priority over careers, family, fame, pleasure, comfort – *everything*.

Take your purity into the world

Although we must focus on developing purity *internally*, avoiding the danger to develop only 'external purity', we must also take our internally developed purity out into the world.

Charles Finney, a famous nineteenth-century American preacher, was extremely averse to this idea. Finney wrote that, after attending a political convention: 'I pray God never to let me go to another. Lies were there; falsehood and ambition were there. I longed to get away alone to pray and to weep.' Even if your first reaction to this is to think this a splendid example of what it means to seek internal purity, let me ask you to reconsider. I would like to suggest that Finney's reaction to the corruptness of politics – which is very common – is actually disastrous. If all Christians adopted such a view what hope would we ever have of being governed justly and fairly? Christians would have no option but to opt out of national politics, local politics and, frankly, out of any sort of management in real life. The results would, of course, be calamitous.

Even the Bible tells us that opting out of the world is not an option. Just a few verses after the Beatitudes Jesus says:

> You are the salt of the earth. But if the salt loses its saltiness, how can it be made salty again? It is no longer good for anything, except to be thrown out and trampled by men. You are the light of the world. A city on a hill cannot be hidden. Neither do people light a lamp and put it under a bowl. Instead they put it on its stand, and it gives light to everyone in the house. In the same way, let your light shine before men, that they may see your good deeds and praise your Father in heaven.
> (Matthew 5:13–16)

In other words, Jesus is expecting His followers to be involved in the world and do their best to make it a better place.

Clearly, we cannot opt out if we want to follow Jesus' advice. We must take the riskier path and walk through a dirty world, while at the same time trying to remain pure. It's logical that this should be the case because if we do manage to maintain any sort of genuine internal purity, it's to be expected that this should motivate our external actions. History has shown that some of the most effective people in the world are people who are most dedicated to keeping themselves pure before God. Doing this isn't easy, but surely that's hardly surprising when we remember that the cross is the symbol of Christianity?

THE PRIZE OF TRUE PURITY: SEEING GOD

Jesus promises us that when we are pure in heart we will *see God.*
No blessing in the Beatitudes is as awesome or as difficult to
comprehend as this! But what exactly are we to make of this little
phrase 'see God'?

Is it possible to see God?

The Church is a faith community born out of the Jewish faith.
Central to Jewish belief was that God was so holy and impossible
to see that no images of Him could be allowed. Yet the early
Christians were adamant that Jesus was God made both visible
and accessible. Paul's statement in the letter to the Colossians
could not be clearer. 'And he [Jesus] is the image of the invisible
God, the firstborn over all creation' (Colossians 1:15). The writer
to the Hebrews says very much the same thing: 'The Son is the
radiance of God's glory and the exact representation of his being,
sustaining all things by his powerful word. After he had provided
purification for sins, he sat down at the right hand of the Majesty
in heaven' (Hebrews 1:3).

Would we survive it?

Intuitively, we are perhaps likely to feel that we could no more
survive seeing the all-powerful, immortal, eternal God than we
could survive a close-up glimpse of the sun. The Bible even confirms
this suspicion and specifically tells us we cannot see God (Exodus
33:20; 1 John 4:12). In terms of power, God is too awesome, too
mighty for us to bear. Indeed, most of the visions of God in the
Bible point out the inadequacy of our senses to see God. Quite
apart from this, God is also far, far holier than even the best of

us. Being even slightly sinful in the presence of the one being in the world who is perfectly sinless involves risking destruction. This may explain why Adam and Eve had to move out of the Garden of Eden (where they enjoyed fellowship with God) after rebelling (Genesis 2:19; 3:8–10). Like the first human beings, we might need to keep our distance from God, simply because we have moved so far away from Him.

What would it involve?

Actually, we may be misleading ourselves by focusing on the strictly visual when interpreting this verse. Even in English we use the word 'see' in a very broad sense. So for instance when someone says, 'I have always wanted to see China,' we know they mean far more than wanting a purely visual experience. They mean they want to be there, to smell the air, feel the sun, and hear the people, birds and animals, eat the food and walk on the soil. The word 'see' is shorthand for 'fully experience'. We can therefore imagine that 'seeing God' might be far more than a visual experience. It must mean knowing Him, becoming acquainted with Him, and having Him close to us.

In the Old Testament God makes a limited number of appearances, almost in every case to people who were very godly. The way these people describe their experiences seems to push language to its very limits. Examples include Moses' glimpse of God (Exodus 33:12–21) and the visions of Isaiah (Isaiah 6:1–13) and Ezekiel (Ezekiel 1:1–28). There are also other gentler, less overpowering appearances of a human figure, such as the one who appears to Abraham (Genesis 18:1–33). Christians have always taken such appearances to be those of Christ before He came in bodily form. These more 'human' appearances of God are exceptions, though, rather than the rule. Usually God is portrayed as being fundamentally distant. In the Old Testament it seems the nearest anyone could get to approaching Him was when the high priest, protected by the sacrificial system, ventured into the total darkness of the deepest interior of the temple.

In the New Testament the situation changes and in Jesus, the invisible God becomes visible. The Word became flesh and dwelt among us (John 1:14). In John's Gospel we read that the night before the crucifixion Philip, one of the disciples, asked Jesus: 'Lord, show us the Father and that will be enough for us.' The answer Jesus gave was extraordinary: 'Don't you know me, Philip, even after I have been among you such a long time? Anyone who has seen me has seen the Father. How can you say, "Show us the Father"? Don't you believe that I am in the Father, and that the Father is in me?' (John 14:8–10). The moment that could be considered the high point of John's Gospel occurs when Thomas, who finally overcomes his doubts, calls the risen Jesus 'my Lord and my God' (John 20:28).

WAYS WE SEE GOD

If we are to understand this promise that we will 'see' God in more than a strictly literal sense, then we must consider the other ways in which the 'pure in heart' will 'see' Him.

We become in awe of God

When this happens, a person no longer experiences God merely in the abstract, as an academic concept discussed by philosophers or theologians. Suddenly, instead of being a mere theoretical concept, God inspires awe. Although we can imagine that people alive during Jesus' earthly life will have had a different kind of access to the divine, in this 'awe-filled' experience of God He is experienced as the utterly overwhelming maker and sustainer of the entire cosmos. It is this kind of experience of God that changes a person's faith, making it acquire a much more profound reality. And we can surmise from people's accounts that this awe-filled experience can be either overwhelming and magnificent or quietly inspiring. However, by all accounts we can conclude that this way of 'seeing God' certainly results in people being changed.

We have access to God

Imagine you have a complaint about something you bought. You go back to the store ready to make your protest and tell an employee at a counter that you want to see the manager. You wouldn't be amused if they pulled out a photograph and said, 'There you are! That's the manager.' The whole point is that you want to have personal contact with the manager. From this we can deduce that the practicality of 'seeing' God must involve having access to Him. In the Middle East and elsewhere in the world, in the past and even today, important people do not make themselves publicly accessible. They hide behind many levels of functionaries and deputies and you end up having to make appointments to make appointments before you get to see them. God, we learn to our astonishment, is not at all like this but is accessible directly, to each and every one of us.

We have an awareness of God

I don't know whether you've ever been out in the countryside with someone who's an authority on wildlife, or gone round a city with someone who is an expert on local history. They're likely to say, 'Look at that!' so as to prompt you to stare at a bird or a building. Even though you see nothing of note and may feel strongly tempted to reply, 'So what?', your companion is then likely to go on to explain what it is you are looking at and why it is significant. In other words, they are likely to help you *see* its significance. The pure in heart are like this with respect to God. They see His hand in the world about them. Whether in personal or global events they see the workings of God. In a world that is frequently full of turmoil and chaos at every level, this is an extraordinarily comforting ability. Whatever crisis erupts they have a quiet and unshakeable confidence that God will work it out according to His own purposes. They are capable of seeing God even in events that most of us would see as being utterly tragic. Those who know God often talk (but never boast) of having known a quiet, comforting joy in the midst of the most terrible of circumstances. Alternatively, they may see miracles in events where other people are likely to simply put things down to 'luck' or coincidence. Either way, this ability to *see* God working in the world is an essential ingredient of happiness.

We see God in the afterlife

We obviously have almost no hard data on visions of God in the afterlife, since the dead are silent. And the Bible says very little on this topic, but we can guess that death involves another experience of 'seeing God'. From the little we have in the Bible on this possibility, we can deduce that death will enable us to see God in a way which is impossible in this life. In the first of his letters, John the apostle says, 'Dear friends, now we are children of God, and what we will be has not yet been made known. But we know that when he appears, we shall be like him, for we shall see him as he is. Everyone who has this hope in him purifies himself, just as he is pure' (1 John 3:2–3). At the end of the book of Revelation we also read: 'No longer will there be any curse. The throne of God and of the Lamb will be in the city, and his servants will serve him. They will see his face, and his name will be on their foreheads' (Revelation 22:3–4). This second passage led many

Roman Catholic theologians in the Middle Ages to spend time speculating on the nature of heaven. They talked about something they called 'the Beatific Vision', the word 'beatific' being related to the Latin word behind the Beatitudes and simply meaning 'blessed'. The idea was that to see God directly and eternally was the ultimate happiness. In God's presence all that affects us now – all misery, pain and anxiety – must disappear. As the rising of the sun vanquishes shadows and gloom so it seems that the appearance of God in all His glory will burn away all that troubles us now. In this view, even the best earthly happiness is temporary in duration, limited in quality and vulnerable in nature. In heaven, on the other hand, in the presence of God, happiness will be eternal, unlimited and invulnerable to change. In fact it will be so different from what we call 'happiness' here that we may be better off abandoning that word and using a greater and shorter word: *joy*.

TO SUM UP

As with all the Beatitudes, the characteristic Jesus praises and the blessings that are promised are linked by cause and effect. Only the pure in heart can see God because they are the only ones whose vision is not clouded. Perhaps it is like a person in an art gallery who examines third-rate paintings, oblivious to the greatness of the other works. Perhaps only people whose hearts are pure are able to perceive the glory and wonder that is God, while the rest of the population are only focused on the problems and mediocrity of life.

Unfortunately, since so many people become mistakenly focused on external aspects of purity, the glory and wonder of God is something that is rarely seen. However, it is evident that if we approach God with the aim of becoming pure to the core, to the very centre of our being, asking for cleansing and forgiveness, the blessing of this beatitude is available to us.

In seeing God in all the ways we've mentioned, we will experience Him in greater fullness than we could ever imagine.

7

Be a Peacemaker

Blessed are the peacemakers,
for they will be called sons of God.
(Matthew 5:9) .

AN ODD BEATITUDE?

I think most people – if asked to pick the odd one out of all the
Beatitudes – would pick this one. It's the only one that explicitly
refers to action, while all the others appear to deal with emotions,
desires and attitudes. This beatitude is also odd in that it singles
out only one of many 'desirable' types of behaviour – peacemaking. Why is this singled out for special attention? Why not
proclaim a blessing on those who feed the poor, on those who
preach the truth? How about people who bring up children, or
look after aged relatives? What about people who give their money
away? We might also legitimately wonder what a peacemaker is
in the first place. Is it someone who works for the UN? A marriage
guidance counsellor? An industrial negotiator? A teacher stepping
in to quell a dispute in a playground? On several counts, blessing
the peacemakers seems a bit odd.

If you have seen the film *Life of Brian* you may remember that
this beatitude is misheard as 'Blessed are the cheesemakers'. Indeed,
because this beatitude seems so out of place, one is almost inclined
to think that some sort of genuine mistake along these lines might
have been made. Perhaps Jesus *was* misheard? Perhaps He meant

something very different? As we look at this beatitude, I think we will see that there is no mistake. Jesus is holding up peacemaking as a central activity for His followers. We will also see that to 'make peace' is a summary of a vast range of good occupations and actions.

WORLDLY DEFINITIONS OF PEACE

Let's start by defining peace. Different people have their own definitions of this word. You might use it to describe a quiet day at the office, as in: 'The boss was away so we had a bit of peace.' You might use it to talk about relationships, as in: 'Tom and Judith have got back together again so there's a bit of peace there.' The word might be applied to some political or international struggle, as in: 'Middle East peace talks resumed today.' Obviously, in general use it's a wide-ranging term and its usage becomes even wider if we imagine what we would come up with if we had to paint or describe a situation that exemplified 'peace'. Would you opt for a beach with the sun setting in a fiery ball, with no other sounds but the lapping of waves and the cries of sea birds? Would you portray 'peace' as a warm, sunlit hill, with long green grass and fluffy white clouds overhead, racing across a clear blue sky? Or would you picture yourself on a winter's evening, sitting in a comfortable chair in front of a warm fire, listening to your favourite music? Undeniably, that kind of peace is valuable, but I'm not sure if it moves us any nearer to a definition of the kind of peace Jesus had in mind.

THE KINDS OF PEACE WE DON'T WANT

Although peace always seems to be a good thing, when we first consider our worldly definitions of peace, we must remember that we are better off without certain types of peace.

Inadequate peace

As we've seen, the idea of 'peace' often conjures up in people's minds the idea of the *absence* of something, rather than the presence of something special. This is certainly the case with 'inadequate' peace. In this type of peace, there is an absence of things like war, hostilities, anger or strain. 'At last I've got some peace,' says the manager as the persistently troublesome client walks out of the office. 'We'll have some peace when he leaves home,' say the parents of a youth who likes to play the drums in his bedroom. On a larger scale the world defines peace as the absence of war. But is this truly adequate? Is peace simply the absence of something nasty happening? Such a definition of peace is essentially negative, like defining love as the absence of antagonism. Wishing or praying for peace surely means a hope for more than merely that the bombing – or the shouting – will stop. The mere ending of pain, hostilities or unpleasantness of whatever sort just signals the beginning of peace. Just as there's more to swimming than not drowning, more to good health than not being ill, more to life than just surviving, so we know there must be more to peace than 'nothing bad happening'.

If nothing else, we can be fairly certain that this kind of negative peace will always be weak, transitory and quite inadequate if we want to survive the onslaught of life's storms. So what are the other types of negative or inadequate peace?

Imposed peace

Imposed peace is achieved by brutality or force. For example we might read in the newspapers, 'After the riot police arrested the troublemakers, the city centre returned to peace.' In Jesus' day much of the civilised world was technically at peace under the rule of Rome, giving rise to the so-called 'Pax Romana'. The Romans even had military medals inscribed with the phrase 'Peace given to the world'. Of course, the reality was that this peace was achieved by crucifying, slaughtering, enslaving or just simply intimidating anybody who might object to Roman rule. In one of his writings, the Roman historian Tacitus refers to Roman attacks in Scotland, writing that 'they make it a desert and call it peace'.

This kind of peace is sadly more common than we might think. You may have experienced (and certainly heard of) families where no one dare answer back to a brutal parent. You may have attended workshops dominated by a bullying manager or worked in offices that are tranquil because of a reign of fear imposed by a tyrannical boss. Most of us would agree that these are not really examples of genuine peace. They lack any sense of justice and fail to give people a sense of security because they aren't likely to feel that peace will be long-lasting. Dissent and disagreement are suppressed, and open wounds of conflict fester and remain septic. History is full of situations where powerful dictatorial leaders have held together warring countries only for the states to disintegrate after their death or removal. The collapses of the Soviet Union or Yugoslavia are cases in point in this respect.

Drugged or 'distracted' peace

In this kind of peace disputes and disagreements are pushed to one side by virtue of drugs or distractions. The drugging may be literal, involving alcohol, cannabis or whatever, or it may be figurative, involving distractions such as television, computer games or incentives. Again, in the case of Rome, many of the emperors allegedly felt that civil unrest was kept at bay by providing 'bread and circuses' for the general population. Modern equivalents are not hard to find – the availability of affordable sporting events, booze and reality TV being obvious examples. One struggling teacher asked a colleague how she managed to get a class to stay quiet. 'Easy,' she said. 'I just give them crayoning to do.' Of course, this is yet another temporary distraction, albeit for a different age group, and certainly doesn't lead to any real peace either.

As with peace that is imposed, peace obtained through drugs or distractions does not last. Drugs wear off and are followed by hangovers or withdrawal symptoms, and disputes start up all over again.

Compromised peace

In this case, peace is obtained only after some kind of unappealing compromise has been reached. For instance, you let your neighbour use your parking slot because he is such a pushy character. Or someone agrees to a child's demands because it's the only way to get any quiet in the household. Peace and quiet result – but not the type that you really want. As somebody once said: 'Another victory like that and we're finished.' People feel they've compromised their values for the sake of a little peace and quiet, so instead of achieving 'peace', they've really only appeased somebody, in all probability only for a short time.

This 'compromised' peace is the type we associate with that fateful meeting in 1938 between Prime Minister Neville Chamberlain and Adolf Hitler. The meeting occurred just after the Nazis had annexed parts of Czechoslovakia and was followed by Chamberlain returning to London, waving a piece of paper in front of the cameras and claiming that he had obtained 'peace in our time'. Of course he hadn't, as we found out over the next seven years.

Sometimes people obtain this kind of peace by bribing a bully. Although it may get the bully off your own back, since you know he's just likely to go off to bully someone else it will just leave you with a bad conscience. In other words, by getting rid of someone undesirable in your life, you gain external peace in exchange for inner turmoil. Thinking back to that meeting which Chamberlain felt had been so successful, we must remember that Hitler soon made further claims and within a year of Chamberlain's negotiations, the world was at war.

Like the other types of undesirable peace we've considered, compromised peace is extremely temporary and holds within it the seeds of destruction. What later erupts might be worse than whatever was staved off supposedly successfully before.

THE BIBLICAL PERSPECTIVE

What does the Bible say about peace? It begins with a state of peace occurring between God and humankind. At the beginning of God's creation, everyone was in perfect harmony with God and with one another – perfect peace on earth. However, within a few pages this precious state has been lost by our rebellion. Very soon peace between people is also over and as early as Chapter 6 of Genesis, we see a record of the first murder. The great writer C. S. Lewis discussed the human realisation that the world is not as it should be. He said, 'If I find in myself a desire which no experience in this world can satisfy, the most probable explanation is that I was made for another world.' Perhaps the story of the Bible is God's active plan to bring His human creation back to the garden – back into full union and peace with Himself.

The rest of the Bible is the long and winding road along which God brings people back to Himself, allowing reconciliation through the incarnation and death of His Son, Jesus Christ. Finally, as you probably know, the Bible ends, in the last chapters of the book of Revelation, with the great and mysterious vision of ultimate and eternal peace restored.

When considering the biblical perspective on peace we must remember the vital fact that peace is always brought about by God's initiative. So active is God in seeking to find peace for human beings that He is described five times in the New Testament letters as 'the God of peace' (Romans 15:33; 16:20; Philippians 4:9; 1 Thessalonians 5:23; Hebrews 13:20). In other words, throughout the Bible we see that while mankind is in dire need of peace, God is the great peacemaker, the one who can show us real peace.

The Old Testament concept of 'shalom'

The word *shalom* is central to the Old Testament concept of peace. It occurs some 250 times throughout the books of the Old Testament and is normally simply translated as 'peace', even though the word really has a much richer meaning than any of the superficially 'nice' meanings we've considered so far.

Firstly, *shalom* has extremely positive connotations. When two people meet and wish each other '*Shalom*' they are not simply saying, 'I hope nothing bad happens to you' or 'I hope you can chill out' – they are communicating much, much more. In uttering the word *shalom* they are saying they wish the other person has everything that is good (for example, prosperity, health, happy relationships) and nothing that is bad (for example, illness, loneliness, poverty).

We are almost given a definition of *shalom* in the Old Testament book of Numbers where we read this great benediction: 'The LORD bless you and keep you; the LORD make his face shine upon you and be gracious to you; the LORD turn his face towards you and give you peace' (Numbers 6:24–26). In other words, everything that is good, everything that a man or woman could want, everything that God can give, is embodied in this little word 'peace'. (Incidentally, did you notice in the above verse the link to the blessing of the previous beatitude? Peace comes when God turns his face towards us; in other words, to see God is to be blessed.)

As we have seen, *shalom* encapsulates the very greatest and richest kind of peace. To fully describe it would mean ransacking the biggest dictionary and thesaurus! We would have to use words like 'harmony', 'well-being', 'good fortune', 'justice' and so on. We would also find ourselves staring at that enticing word that lies at the core of this book: happiness. In a very real sense, having *shalom* means enjoying true happiness. In today's marketing language *shalom* is not just peace, it is 'peace plus'. Unlike the inadequate type of peace we discussed earlier, there is nothing lacking in the peace described by the Old Testament word *shalom*.

As well as having a very broad meaning, *shalom* also has a sense of moral depth because it is inescapably linked with both righteousness and justice. It would not be *shalom* for the villain to walk away quietly and peacefully into the sunset, for the poor to be left to starve or for the dispossessed to live out their existence as refugees in a country only officially at peace. The concept must also embrace righteousness! This moral backbone to *shalom* acts as an antidote to the bad types of peace we discussed earlier. It has absolutely nothing in common with 'imposed', 'drugged', 'distracted' or 'compromised' peace. And precisely because the *shalom* version of peace is based on justice, fairness and righteousness it has the potential to endure. Beyond this, it's also encouraging to note that the Old Testament definition of peace (encapsulated in the word *shalom*) is not just an ideal to dream of and pray for – it's something which we are told to actively seek out. In the psalms we read: 'Turn from evil and do good; seek peace and pursue it' (Psalm 34:14).

On the negative side, if you see it that way, the concept of *shalom* is only applied to God's chosen people, Israel, and it is also limited in time – at most to a human lifetime, and frequently less. It's somewhat perplexing, in fact, that the Jewish people so rarely seemed to attain *shalom*: it was only briefly enjoyed on a national level during the reign of Solomon – whose name, incidentally, is related to the word *shalom*. This peace, involving unity, prosperity and security for all Israel, lasted for no more than a couple of decades during the ninth century BC (during the early part of Solomon's reign) and constituted the pinnacle of Old Testament history. Only during this brief period did Israel become a world power and live out its calling to be a light to the Gentiles. As we read in 1 Kings 4:20–25:

> The people of Judah and Israel were as numerous as the sand on the seashore; they ate, they drank and they were happy. And Solomon ruled over all the kingdoms from the River to the land of the Philistines, as far as the border of Egypt. These countries brought tribute and were Solomon's subjects all his life. Solomon's daily provisions were thirty cors of fine flour and sixty cors of meal, ten head of stall-fed cattle, twenty of pasture-fed cattle and a hundred sheep and goats, as well as deer, gazelles, roebucks and choice fowl. For he ruled over all the kingdoms west of the River, from Tiphsah to Gaza, and had peace on all sides. During Solomon's lifetime Judah and Israel, from Dan to Beersheba, lived in safety, each man under his own vine and fig-tree.

However amusing the details, from this account we definitely get the idea that there was peace on all sides; then, as soon as it had begun, it was all over. Solomon made unwise marriages and allowed forays into what we would call 'multi-faith worship' and soon religious, political and economic decline set in. Within a generation, the kingdom was divided and at war internally and externally. The following century saw the Jewish nation almost (but not quite) disintegrate to the point of being obliterated from history. From then on, for eight centuries, we find accounts of a wistful longing for that great and fleeting feeling of *shalom*.

It seems to me that this is representative of all human experience of peace. No sooner do we experience it than it slips away, like a beautiful scene receding in the rear-view mirror. Isn't this how most of us experience happiness? All this would seem very bleak if it were not for the promise contained in the Old Testament – the promise of a Messiah.

THE IDEA OF PEACE RESTORED BY A MESSIAH

Over and again the Old Testament promise is of the coming of a Messiah, who would bring peace and save Israel. Things had become so bad in the nation's experience that the idea of any kind of peace must have seemed a joke, but somehow the hope of a real and lasting *shalom* in the future had begun to come into focus. Prophecies about the Messiah typically emphasised two angles. First, the Messiah was seen as a king in the line of David and Solomon, who would be gifted with superhuman powers that would allow him to push back borders and crush the nation's enemies. Second, this Messiah was seen as less triumphal than a regular king. He was portrayed as being a servant who was going to suffer for the nation. Interestingly, from our perspective, both of these strands of prophecy were associated with peace.

In order to understand the significance of the Old Testament prophecies centring on these two themes, let's review them. Some of them will be familiar from Christmas services or Handel's *Messiah* but others will probably be less well known to you.

Prince of Peace!

Isaiah writes:

> For to us a child is born,
>   to us a son is given,
>   and the government will be on his shoulders.
> And he will be called
>   Wonderful Counsellor, Mighty God,
>   Everlasting Father, Prince of Peace.
> Of the increase of his government and peace
>   there will be no end.
> He will reign on David's throne
>   and over his kingdom,
> establishing and upholding it
>   with justice and righteousness
>   from that time on and forever.
> The zeal of the LORD Almighty will accomplish this.
> (Isaiah 9:6–7)

Did you catch that vital double reference to peace?

Peace brought through punishment

Later in Isaiah, in one of the great passages to do with the coming servant we read: 'But he was pierced for our transgressions, he was crushed for our iniquities; the punishment that brought us peace was upon him, and by his wounds we are healed' (Isaiah 53:5). Suddenly, this prince of peace was to be visualised suffering – in a no doubt puzzling or incomprehensible way, especially for those outside the Christian faith.

Peace brought personally

In Micah 5:1–5 we find a hint that this Messiah will somehow *personally* bring peace:

> Marshal your troops, O city of troops,
>> for a siege is laid against us.
> They will strike Israel's ruler
>> on the cheek with a rod.
> But you, Bethlehem Ephrathah,
>> though you are small among the clans of Judah,
> out of you will come for me
>> one who will be ruler over Israel,
> whose origins are from of old,
>> from ancient times.
> Therefore Israel will be abandoned
>> until the time when she who is in labour gives birth
> and the rest of his brothers return
>> to join the Israelites.
> He will stand and shepherd his flock
>> in the strength of the LORD,
>> in the majesty of the name of the LORD his God.
> And they will live securely, for then his greatness
>> will reach to the ends of the earth.
>> And he will be their peace.

This must have been mystifying to people at the time it was written because there is no later explanation in the Old Testament as to how this kind of peace would occur. Yet the passage implies that we will actually be the embodiment of *shalom*, with the help of the Messiah.

THE NEW TESTAMENT EXPLANATION

If the writers of the Old Testament were unable to resolve the mystery of the Messiah (somehow both king and servant, ruler and sufferer), the writers of the New Testament have a clearer view. They realised, no doubt initially through their first-hand experience, that the Messiah had come in the form of Jesus and that He had brought peace with Him.

The messages about peace actually came quickly in the New Testament. At the birth of Jesus the armies of heaven appear to the shepherds 'praising God and saying, "Glory to God in the highest, and on earth peace to men on whom his favour rests" '(Luke 2:14). Jesus' coming to earth was a sign that God's *shalom* is being poured out onto all humanity, although initially it was only seen as being targeted at the Jewish people. However, Jesus was, and still is, the peacemaker *par excellence*. He talked about peace and peacemaking both directly and indirectly and an essential and revolutionary part of His teaching was the idea of unconditional forgiveness – making peace that much easier to achieve. He took this even further in the Sermon on the Mount, when He advised people to go beyond the justice of the past and not only be generous in terms of forgiving, but also in order to build bridges. As we know, He said:

> You have heard that it was said, 'Eye for eye, and tooth for tooth.' But I tell you, do not resist an evil person. If someone strikes you on the right cheek, turn to him the other also. And if someone wants to sue you and take your tunic, let him have your cloak as well. If someone forces you to go one mile, go with him two miles. Give to the one who asks you, and do not turn away from the one who wants to borrow from you.
>
> You have heard that it was said, 'Love your neighbour and

hate your enemy.' But I tell you: Love your enemies and pray for those who persecute you, that you may be sons of your Father in heaven. He causes his sun to rise on the evil and the good, and sends rain on the righteous and the unrighteous. If you love those who love you, what reward will you get? Are not even the tax collectors doing that? And if you greet only your brothers, what are you doing more than others? Do not even pagans do that? Be perfect, therefore, as your heavenly Father is perfect. (Matthew 5:38–48)

Of course, this teaching was in stark contrast to the teaching of the Old Testament, where retribution was readily permitted. Most of us are familiar with the famous – or infamous! – principle of 'an eye for an eye, a tooth for a tooth' that Jesus mentions here. He was effectively annulling this and challenging the whole idea of retaliation, thereby removing an enormous obstacle to peace-making. We need to remember that Jesus did not say this in some idyllic country at a time when retaliation was a purely theoretical issue, but at a time when the Jewish nation was under brutal occupation. Even in this atmosphere, Jesus rejected all bitterness and retribution and taught about ways of bringing peace instead.

Jesus' use of the word 'peace' is particularly striking because He clearly sees it as not only something that is wished upon others (as when someone says, '*Shalom*') but also as a thing that He was uniquely able to give away. This is clear in two verses in John's Gospel:

Peace I leave with you; my peace I give you. I do not give to you as the world gives. Do not let your hearts be troubled and do not be afraid. (John 14:27)

I have told you these things, so that in me you may have peace. In this world you will have trouble. But take heart! I have overcome the world. (John 16:33)

Later we read that during at least four of the resurrection appearances Jesus introduced Himself with the words 'Peace be with you' (Luke 24:36; John 20:19; 20:21; 20:26). The fact that this phrase is recorded is surely an indication that we are meant to see it as more than just a greeting. In the book of Acts, Jesus is even more explicitly linked with the coming of peace. In Acts 10:36, for example, we read: 'You know the message God sent to the people of Israel, telling the good news of peace through Jesus Christ, who is Lord of all.' It therefore seems clear that Jesus was both peace-*maker* and peace-*giver.*

Moving on through Jesus' life on earth, we then come to His death on the cross. The precise link between this and the bringing of peace is only hinted at in the Gospels, although it is extensively developed in the rest of the New Testament. Paul's letters, in particular, are full of peace, and often begin with the twin blessing 'grace and peace'. It is perhaps Paul who best summarises what Jesus did on earth, writing in one of his letters: 'For God was pleased to have all his fullness dwell in him [i.e. in Jesus], and through him to reconcile to himself all things, whether things on earth or things in heaven, by making peace through his blood, shed on the cross' (Colossians 1:20). Christ's death was a cosmic act of peacemaking.

We therefore see how extraordinarily wide-ranging the New Testament depiction of peace is. It is peace which reunites God with men and women on earth. This is neatly summarised in Romans 5:1: 'Therefore, since we have been justified through faith, we have peace with God through our Lord Jesus Christ.' Yet it is also peace that embraces people laterally, as it were, because it enables human beings to become at peace with each other. Talking about the great divide between Jew and Gentile, Paul says:

For he [Jesus] himself is our peace, who has made the two one and has destroyed the barrier, the dividing wall of hostility, by abolishing in his flesh the law with its commandments and regulations. His purpose was to create in himself one new man out of the two, thus making peace, and in this one body to reconcile both of them to God through the cross, by which he put to death their hostility. He came and preached peace to you who were far away and peace to those who were near. For through him we both have access to the Father by one Spirit. (Ephesians 2:14–18)

Through this and the many other references to peace in the New Testament we learn that peace is one of the great blessings available to us in Jesus. Sometimes the whole idea of peace seems to sum up everything that was gained for us through Christ, as is expressed in Philippians 4:7: 'And the peace of God, which transcends all understanding, will guard your hearts and your minds in Christ Jesus.'

A GIFT TO BE ACCEPTED

Before we go on to consider what kind of peacemakers Jesus might have been talking about in this beatitude, it's important to remember that the peace He brings needs to be accepted, if everything else is to fall into place. Peace may have been bought at the cross and offered freely to humankind, but it is still only a *gift* and even gifts can be rejected. Even in His life on earth, Jesus implied that rejecting Him would mean rejecting peace. For example, in Luke 19:41–44 we read:

As he approached Jerusalem and saw the city, he wept over it and said, 'If you, even you, had only known on this day what would bring you peace – but now it is hidden from your eyes. The days will come upon you when your enemies will build an embankment against you and encircle you and hem you in on every side. They will dash you to the ground, you and the children within your walls. They will not leave one stone on another, because you did not recognise the time of God's coming to you.'

Here Jesus prophesied that Jerusalem's dismissal of Him would be a rejection of God's coming, and that this would inevitably result in a loss of peace.

A tragic but inevitable side-effect of Jesus being the one who brings peace is the fact that He therefore becomes a focus of division. This is why Jesus said (as is recorded in Matthew 10:34): 'Do not suppose that I have come to bring peace to the earth. I did not come to bring peace, but a sword.' You often hear people say of someone that (a bit like Marmite) you 'either love them or hate them'. Well, such a phrase was never truer than with Jesus. Yes, He had, and still has, adoring followers. However, there have also been those who have rejected Him to the point of hatred.

WHAT KIND OF PEACE?

In this beatitude, Jesus asks us to *make* peace, not simply keep it, or love it whenever it happens to be around. This beatitude does not say 'Blessed are the peace-lovers' or even 'Blessed are the peace-keepers', but 'Blessed are the peace-*makers*'. Almost everybody, from presidents to pop stars, is in favour of peace, so it's easy to be a peace-*lover*. What we need to consider is how we can become people who actively *create* peace. If any of us are confused by the similarities in English between the words 'pacify' and 'passive' we need to have a serious rethink! After all, pacifying someone often involves hard or dangerous work and being a peacemaker is similarly active.

This idea is confirmed in the New Testament, where we find repeated references to the need for us to work for peace. For example, in Hebrews 12:14 we read: 'Work at living in peace with everyone, and work at living a holy life, for those who are not holy will not see the Lord' (NLT). In the letter from James we read: 'But the wisdom that comes from heaven is first of all pure; then peace-loving, considerate, submissive, full of mercy and good fruit, impartial and sincere. Peacemakers who sow in peace raise a harvest of righteousness' (James 3:17–18). Another comment Paul makes to the church in Corinth summarises all that peace-making involves: 'Dear brothers and sisters, I close my letter with these last words: Be joyful. Grow to maturity. Encourage each other. Live in harmony and peace. Then the God of love and peace will be with you' (2 Corinthians 13:11, NLT). I think it is also significant that in a number of places the Holy Spirit is linked with peace. In Romans 14:17 we read: 'For the kingdom of God is not a matter of eating and drinking, but of righteousness, peace and joy in the Holy Spirit.' In Galatians 5:22–23 we find: 'The fruit of the Spirit is love, joy, peace, patience, kindness, goodness, faithfulness.'

Note too that hidden in that innocent little word 'peacemaker' lies the call to seek justice, honesty, decency, fairness and prosperity. Behind that tiny word is a reminder to think positively about achieving good, rather than pondering on how to simply confound evil. Being a peacemaker means not simply trying to end conflict (although that is no bad thing), but actually bringing blessing to the world. Much, perhaps all, of what we would categorise as doing good – helping the poor, feeding the hungry, defending the weak and even saving the environment – could be considered part of 'making peace'. Being a peacemaker means doing what we can to bring heaven to earth. Whenever Christ's followers counter evil, whether it's ending the exploitation of women and children, the liberation of people from drugs or alcohol, the tidying up of the neighbourhood, or just helping people get through the day, they are fulfilling this beatitude.

Do you now understand why Jesus sees the people who make these things happen as being blessed?

WHERE TO MAKE PEACE?

We should aim to achieve peace in every possible area of our lives, in every possible way. In other words, I think we should pursue peace between people and God, between family and neighbour and between nations. Thinking about this in terms of concentric circles, starting at the core and moving outwards, we see that our peacemaking should begin where we are.

Begin with yourself

Perhaps surprisingly, I think the first person you may need to make peace with is yourself. Many of us are fragmented and divided people. We don't really know who we are or what we want and much of the time we don't really like ourselves. We exist in a state of low-level internal conflict. While I'm not suggesting we all have split personalities in the strict psychological sense, there are all too often warring factions within us. For instance, one part of us may want to be bold and brave while the other part is timid; one part is a dreamy optimist and the other is a deadly cynic. Frequently, we find ourselves standing in judgement on some aspect of our lives. We might hear ourselves saying: 'That was a ridiculous thing to do!', 'I never get it right!' or 'I'm such a failure!' Some people seem to be able to stare in the mirror and feel loathing at what they see. Often as not, what is driving this feeling is not genuine feelings of guilt but simply self-critical feelings of worthlessness. (And to remind you of the theme of this book, nothing is more likely to prevent an outbreak of happiness than perpetual, nagging self-criticism.)

If this sounds like you, you must reconsider and re-establish your relationship with God. It's strange how one of the most frequent criticisms of Christianity is its preoccupation with the idea of God as judge. This is particularly remarkable given that, as far as I can make out, most people live under judgement already, from themselves rather than from God. In fact, it's far better to replace that vicious, unpredictable and unforgiving inner judge with one who has clearly set down the basis for forgiveness. If you genuinely regret what you've done wrong and wish to live a new and better life, then God offers you permanent forgiveness through Jesus Christ. And of course it doesn't stop there: with God's forgiveness comes adoption into His family. We can never again say that we're worthless if we understand we're now part of the royal family! If God has accepted and forgiven us then we can surely both accept and forgive ourselves. Those who become Christians know the experience of God's Spirit moving into their lives and one of His tasks is to assure us of our identity and worth as God's children.

In other words, the foundation stone of peacemaking is to be at peace with God. My job title is 'evangelist' and I like this because it seems to me that being an evangelist means being someone who encourages this most fundamental of all forms of peace: that between people and God. Indeed, the Christian message can be stated like this: God wants you to have peace with Him through Jesus. I can't tell you about this need too strongly. Becoming reconciled with God generates an enormous power and strength, which is a great asset in peacemaking. As people who are forgiven we should be able to forgive others; and as people who have known the blessing of peace, we should be enthusiastic about giving that peace away.

So knowing this peace is absolutely central to any peacemaking efforts you might make. And it's readily available thanks to Christ's death on the cross – as long as it's personally accepted.

Move out to family and friends

The next step, after making peace yourself with God, is to make peace with everyone in your own family, and with everybody with whom you come into contact. It's all too tempting to want to rush out into the wider world before doing this, but that really would be counter-productive. At least for the time being, forget about work colleagues who scowl at each other; forget about the gangs in your town who are involved in endless scuffles; even forget, just for a moment, those many places around the world where people are at war with each other. You can earn the Nobel Peace Prize later, but first please remember that peacemaking begins at home! Imagine how bizarre it would seem to outsiders for an international peacemaker to be at war with his neighbours. Imagine how inconsistent and unconvincing it would seem for a politician involved in international peacemaking to be involved in a legal battle with colleagues.

Actually, it may well be much harder and more painful to make peace at home than it is to make it far away. After all, when your central African peace mission fails, you can shrug your shoulders, get on a plane home and leave the wreckage behind. Not so with family and friends, but this mustn't stop us from trying. We need to try every possible method we can think of in our particular situation and never give up! If we are having trouble creating peace with our husband or wife, we must remember that in Malachi 2:16 it says that God hates divorce. (Later, in Matthew 19:7–9, we learn that Jesus also emphasised that this is not the best way.) If we are having problems with our children or friends, even if a path to resolution and harmony is long, tiresome and painful, we must persevere, remembering that progress is likely to be made in tiny steps, rather than giant leaps. We must also remember that we have the power of the Holy Spirit to help us in all our difficulties. When we have achieved a good level of peace in our domestic and social situation then and only then should we look outwards, always reminding ourselves to look inwards to check on our own relationship with God and others.

Make peace within society

Sadly, most of us live and work in settings where there is tension. Stress is often expressed in anger against others, and then bitterness is born. But if we're serious about following Jesus Christ, then we need to become peacemakers in our workplaces and communities as well as in our homes.

However, first of all we need to understand why we avoid trying to create peace between the people around us. There are perhaps two key reasons why we often just stand by and let disputes happen. One is quite simply that other people's squabbles can actually be quite amusing. We may have abolished blood sports, but many of us still find it perversely enjoyable watching the utterly predictable way in which neighbours and colleagues unleash attacks on each other. We've probably all been at meetings where, as old enemies begin launching salvos of familiar accusations at each other, we see knowing glances of quiet pleasure on the faces of the observers. The other reason for ducking any attempt at peacemaking is simply fear. We all know that peacemakers get hurt and that if you try to separate fighting dogs you're likely to get bitten yourself. Regular news stories of shootings or stabbings of innocent parties who tried to bring resolution to a dispute prove this point.

Despite our natural reluctance to intervene in other people's disputes and help them find peaceful resolution, we really must intervene and help if we are to take Jesus' teachings seriously. In this respect, you may be reassured to remember that peacemaking often involves more than simply intervening at a time of crisis – it could often involve preventing hostilities in the first place so that disputes can be avoided altogether. It's so much easier to prevent an accident than to treat the consequences with emergency surgery! In other words, by simply trying to spot potential areas of conflict before they erupt we may help people around us avoid all kinds of problems. In this respect, perhaps we should remember the words of Proverbs 12:6: 'The words of the wicked lie in wait for blood, but the speech of the upright rescues them,' and also of Proverbs 10:21, where we read: 'The lips of the righteous nourish many, but fools die for lack of judgment.'

So whatever the reasons for our own reluctance, if we want to be peacemakers, we must find the courage to help people around us. We must not accept low-level warfare and tolerate strife in our day-to-day lives – we must do all that we possibly can to heal rifts so that other people can also enjoy the benefits promised both through the word *shalom* in the Old Testament and through the promise of a Messiah in the New Testament. After all, why should we keep all the benefits of peace only for ourselves?

Beyond an involvement with local and national campaigns we also need to consider various ethical questions. For example, we need to decide what we personally can do to express our disapproval of organisations who make money out of war. Even if we accept the logic that wars will always exist, that they need to be fought, and therefore that there must be a defence industry, as most of us probably do, can we really also accept the price tag? Can we not do something to counter the celebration and blatant marketing of war? Can we not also campaign for money to be allocated more wisely and for decisions to be made on a more Christian basis? Personally, I find it profoundly troubling that such a high proportion of our nation's wealth comes from the defence industries. In the UK some 400,000 people are employed by the aerospace and defence industries. What's more, weapons are sold to individuals and nations on an almost uncontrolled basis world-wide. As followers of Jesus, can we really view this situation with anything less than dismay? And should our dismay not prompt us to action?

One inspiring example of a company who made a stand is one of Denmark's most famous companies, Lego. For deeply held moral reasons the makers of the almost universal children's building toys have long refused to give in to the enormous market pressure to produce a military version of their toys. Good for them! We need to look carefully at our own commitments and investments. Could we make a similar stand?

We also need to ask hard and penetrating questions of our political leaders and the press. For followers of Jesus Christ, war is always a very last resort. It is the moral equivalent of drastic surgery, to be employed only when all other options have failed. At the very least, we need to be sure that all other options have been tried. We also need to force our leaders to look beyond the glib clichés of 'surgical strikes', 'quick clean wars' or 'regime change' to the harsh realities that are involved. It will not be easy. The nature of the human race is such that we find making war a lot easier than making peace so we, as Christians, need to encourage others through the more painful process of peacemaking.

Finally, when considering this issue, we need to remember that making peace always stretches well beyond simply stopping fighting and engaging in simple conflict resolution. A fundamental part of peacemaking involves encouraging true bridge-building between peoples, resulting in harmony not conflict. Historians tell us that the seeds of the Second World War were sown in the vindictive peace settlement of Versailles that followed the end of the First World War, and which caused enormous German resentment. Apparently, on seeing the terms of the Versailles Treaty, the French Field Marshal Ferdinand Foch said, 'This is not peace. It is an armistice for twenty years.' This was, unfortunately, an uncannily accurate prediction. He turned out to be incorrect by a mere two months. Had peace-making in the biblical sense taken place at that time, the disastrous war from 1939 to 1945 might well have been avoided. Furthermore, if the end of that conflict had been marked by better peace-making then the poisoned landscape that is the current Middle East might have been avoided. In other words, we shouldn't be heeding the advice of the political adviser who in the latter years of the Roman Empire, wrote: 'If you want peace, prepare for war.' While that may have some military virtue, a wiser rule for life is, 'If you want peace, then make preparations for peace.' After all, as we've seen, peacemaking involves far more than simply putting out fires; it means creating environments in which fires cannot start in the first place.

SOME PRACTICAL TIPS

Here are a few personal suggestions for approaches you might want to take in peace-making. Consider each of the 'peace-making activities' in your own life and decide which of the following principles apply, or are useful to you.

Treat peace as valuable

In a world that is cynical about almost everything, we need to be careful that we actively celebrate peace and show no cynicism ourselves. By the effort we invest in bringing about peace, we also need to demonstrate to people how valuable we regard it to be.

Hopefully, you will naturally do this, having been made aware from the media and your general experience of life how devastating a *lack* of peace can be, both geo-politically and domestically. On a domestic level, if you know anything about your own family history, you will almost always know about some incidence of hostility. You know the sort of thing: 'Uncle George had a row with Uncle Billy and they didn't speak to each other for thirty years.' Marriages break up, people are forced to move house, enormous damage is inflicted on children, lives are cut short through anxiety and argument and this all takes place because of a lack of peace. Talk to a dozen people about their jobs and at least five of them will say things like, 'It would be fine if it weren't for my colleagues', 'It would be great if I didn't have to spend so much time on riot control in the classroom' or 'It would be the perfect job, if there wasn't so much infighting among the management.' As you must know, even this most limited level of conflict stains and damages life. Whatever is the cost of all this lack of peace at the social level? What is the price to the nation of broken marriages? Of stress at work? Of the estimated 4.5 million CCTV cameras that are operating in Britain alone?

At every level, personal, social and global, peace has enormous benefits. Therefore, in everything we do, we must help to make other people aware of these, so that they too will come to value peace and strive to attain it.

Consider it an investment

It's easy to see how peace can be a real investment, if we remember how many problems are caused in any situation where peace is lacking. Just as money saved or invested comes in handy in times of need, so too investment in peace later brings about unforeseen benefits. Imagine that two people work for the same company. One day, one of them annoys the other by accidentally scratching his car in the company car park. This is far less likely to result in a real problem if the two of them have built up a friendly relationship beforehand. The same applies in other areas of life. Like a car, if you keep your relationships in good repair there is much less chance they will stop working properly, or conk out on you altogether. If the *shalom* bank balance can be kept positive, you are much less likely to get overdrawn.

Much of this kind of 'investment' peacemaking can almost become a way of life. Make friends, build up your friendships, and encourage other people to be friends and share with each other. You'll continually reap the benefits of this way of living. After all, this approach is so much easier than the alternative, which is to ignore relationships until they demand attention because of what could otherwise have been a relatively small hitch. Without the right kind of foundation, even the tiniest niggle can destroy a relationship that had the potential to flower. Often rescuing it at that stage is *really* hard work. Rather than heeding the cynical comment about conflicts, which says that you should 'always get your revenge in first', we need to heed the advice which has infinitely more wisdom: *get your peacemaking in first!*

Make peace wisely

Although our goal should always be to 'make peace', we should not do this foolishly, or simply for short-term gain. We need to work towards a long-term peace, which upholds justice and reflects our deeply held, God-given principles, as taught in the Bible. The peace that the wife achieves by giving in to the abusive husband is not only short-sighted and weak, it is wrong. The same applies to the superficial and tenuous peace achieved by a nation which gives in to an invading oppressor. The 'peace and quiet' achieved by a teacher giving in to rebellious pupils is also both foolish and misguided because it does nothing to enhance the general education of the pupils.

Having said this, we must also acknowledge that there are times when being wise involves being assertive. To stand by when a bully is beating someone up actually amounts to being an accessory to injustice.

In the Old Testament book of Ecclesiastes, there is a great list of parallel statements that begins, 'There is a time for everything, and a season for every activity under heaven: a time to be born and a time to die, a time to plant and a time to uproot . . .' The list ends with 'a time for war and a time for peace' (Ecclesiastes 3:1–8). This is certainly the case, and deciding when to 'make peace', perhaps by taking some difficult action or asserting oneself, is something we need to decide with much wisdom. The good news is that Jesus has not left us alone. God has sent His Holy Spirit to be our counsellor and guide (John 14:15–21). We can trust the Lord, knowing that whenever we ask for wisdom, He will provide it. James wrote, 'If any of you lacks wisdom, he should ask God, who gives generously to all without finding fault, and it will be given to him' (James 1:5–6). I suggest that we pray, whenever we are in doubt, and also seek the best possible advice available to us, so as to decide on a right course of action. We must do this as persistently and as sincerely as we can, taking whatever action we eventually decide is necessary, because that 'right' kind of peace is worth making the effort for.

Unlike the kind of peace that is attained 'unwisely', a wisely won peace will endure and eventually bring true happiness to everyone concerned. In other words, although justice may hurt in the early stages, it will at least allow the foundations to be laid for a more lasting and fulfilling peace.

Be a gracious peacemaker

One of the most important Christian virtues required in order to be an effective peacemaker is *grace*. Grace allows a person to start out from a position of humility, with the realisation that any effort expended will not bring personal fame and fortune. While the peacemaking itself may well be effective, it is highly unlikely to bring any great accolades. (Bang goes that Nobel Peace Prize after all!) In fact, peacemaking is often a thankless task. You see, you can't really boast about peacemaking without risking undoing all the good work you've already done. If you have, after much effort, brought together A and B over some major difficulty, then you need to ensure that they forget that any unpleasantness ever existed. One of the worst possible things you can do is to actually remind the world that this difficulty between A and B existed, because that might open up old wounds all over again and effectively provoke A or B to revive and continue their original dispute. In order for the differences to be forgotten, the act of peacemaking may have to be forgotten too. Consequently, if you were the person responsible for resolving a conflict, or for preventing any conflict occurring in the first place, you'll also be totally forgotten. Little wonder, then, that peacemakers need to be humble.

Empathise!

Putting yourself in the other person's shoes is always an essential element of successful peacemaking. After all, how can you decide the appropriate thing to do if you can't imagine how the other person feels? We need to *empathise*.

If you can somehow identify with both sides in a conflict, or potential conflict, so that each party relates to you effectively, there will be a much higher chance of success. This is simply because the channels of communication will be opened up and what might begin with small snippets of personal information may well develop into full-blown, harmonious communication, not just with you but also with the other person who was previously felt to be 'the enemy'. It is no accident that Christians have always identified Jesus as the perfect peacemaker between humankind and God because as perfect man and perfect God

He was able to represent both parties: Jesus was the perfect go-between, and the perfect mediator.

If both sides relate well to the peacemaker they may see something of themselves in him or her, but on the negative side they may instead identify them with their enemy. Indeed, all too often a peacemaker may be mistaken for a foe. While this is unfortunate, it is not something that should put you off making peace. It is merely yet another thing to be aware of if you want to enjoy success.

Cultivate some other essential qualities

Although we have touched upon many essential elements of effective peacemaking, we have not yet considered all the qualities we need to develop in order to be an effective peacemaker.

Be loving

We have not yet mentioned the great Christian virtue of love. I hope, by now, it is obvious how vital love is in any peacemaking efforts. We really need to *care* about people we wish to make peace with or between because no other strategies will ever be as powerful as a caring approach. If you doubt this, consider for a moment how ineffective machines would be at peacemaking. While they can perform increasingly complex tasks I very much doubt they will ever be effective at making peace, simply because of the essential ingredients of love and care.

Learn to cope with stress

If we learn how to handle stress without getting ruffled, we will certainly be much more effective. In resolving conflict you are dealing with difficult situations and strained people, so it is extremely helpful if you can remain in control of your own stress. After all, people who are involved in disputes, or who are on the verge of a dispute, are in a delicate state. If we handle our own stress poorly, perhaps confiding in a third party inappropriately, the original dispute which involved 'only' two people might quickly extend to include the third party!

To understand this even better, we just need to consider a nuclear reactor. Control rods are a key element in their construction. These are columns of substances like graphite that have the property of absorbing radiation flying about inside the reactor. The control rods enable the reactors to operate safely by preventing them from getting dangerously overheated. Peacemakers need to have something of that quality: the ability to be in a situation, absorbing any dangerous and potentially explosive radiation. While peacemakers hear accusations about other people, or even themselves, they need to be able to nod quietly and sympathetically, while also quelling the accusation and allowing it to go no further. The value of people with such gifts is often underestimated.

Be tactful and patient

Of course, these are also key qualities to effective peacemaking. We need to sense raw nerves and carefully avoid touching them. If we are to be successful in making peace, we need to soothe battered egos, without taking sides.

Clearly, there are also many other gifts that we must seek in order to be effective peacemakers. According to one dictionary I consulted, we need to learn the arts of conciliation, negotiation, appreciation and co-operation. This dictionary also suggested avoiding the vices of agitation, alienation, irritation, exaggeration, domination and humiliation.

Be realistic

Finally – having considered things largely from a positive perspective, we need to recognise our limitations in terms of successful peacemaking. The Bible's view is that both the world and the human race are severely damaged. This means it will only be possible to achieve perfect peace – that great *shalom* – when Jesus returns in power and glory. Not until then will everything be truly made right and a final, perfect and eternal peace be brought about. At that time the spiritual peace for His followers that Jesus made possible on the cross will become a physical, psychological and spiritual peace for all creation. Until then we must do our best, while realising that any peace we achieve is bound to be temporary and limited. Even the best victories of our peacemaking will be, if you like, no more than the first instalments of God's great and eternal peace. Such triumphs are well worth working for but are not to be confused with the real thing, which is still to come. Of course, that's another reason to be humble.

TO SUM UP

As with the other beatitudes, peacemaking is richly rewarded. While the effort and limited success rate might cost us dearly, we can still be reassured by the blessing Jesus promised. In a way, these blessings give us an incentive to make an effort. It's as if Jesus was saying that although being a peacemaker means standing in no man's land between the warring parties and risking being shot at by both sides, it's worth the risk! After all, as we've seen, 'peace' is a shorthand word for every blessing we can imagine. Bringing peace in the full sense of the Hebrew word *shalom* means bringing the greatest possible good to people around us. There is no higher praise that can be bestowed on us than that 'we brought peace'. There is no safer route to happiness than through the power and grace of Jesus. After all, by bringing peace and consequently happiness to other people, we will inevitably experience greater happiness ourselves. This is because of something we haven't mentioned before – happiness is quite simply contagious!

What is the blessing, though? To modern ears it sounds rather strange and possibly even sexist: 'For they will be called sons of God.' We are probably better off translating this as 'children of God', yet we need to consider the original phrase in the light of its cultural context. Exploring what 'sons of God' meant in Jesus' original usage illuminates the richness of blessing Jesus meant for all of God's children – men and women alike.

In the culture of Jesus' time, this phrase was used in the context of *inheritance*, as it still is in some Middle Eastern societies today. In families where there are several wives, a distinction is made between a man's 'boys' (by a second wife) and his 'sons' (by his main wife). All are his children, but the *sons* are special and they alone are the heirs, the inheritors and the ones who, it is hoped, will continue the family line. So to be a son is to have something of the authority of the father. A friend of mine who has travelled much in the Arab world tells of going to a remote village where he needed a document signed by the headman, the sheikh. He was dismayed to be told that the man had left and wouldn't be back for days. The locals, however, rebuked his disappointment. 'Oh it doesn't matter,' they said. 'The son of the sheikh is here.' In their eyes the son had all the authority that the father had. So I think one aspect of being a son of God is knowing something of the authority and power that God has. It means being 'very special'.

A second cultural concept relating to sonship in Jesus' time concerns *intimacy*. Having a son and father relationship meant being very close indeed. From the son's point of view, there were no barriers between himself and his father; the door was always open. From the father's point of view, nothing was normally hidden from the son. They were 'family' in the deepest and best sense of the word.

The third relevant idea concerns *identity*. In the culture in which Jesus was preaching, calling someone 'a son of' someone suggested that the person bore the character of their father. For example, when Jesus described John and James as being 'the sons of thunder' (in Mark 3:17) he was not referring to some bizarre myth about their parentage, but was recognising that they had the fierce and unpredictable characteristics of thunder. So in this beatitude being 'a son of God' means that we share God's character. As we have seen, this is appropriate because being a peacemaker means doing what God has been doing since the dawn of human history. Imagine the feeling that an adopted child must get when someone, unaware of the child's adopted status, says admiringly, 'You're just like your father.' There can be no higher praise for us than for people to say, 'You're acting just like God.'

So to be called 'sons of God' expresses all three ideas: we inherit God's authority, we have intimacy with God as our heavenly Father and we share something of God's character. Clearly, this rich blessing for the peacemakers is well worth working for.

8

Don't Worry if You are Persecuted

Blessed are those who are persecuted
because of their righteousness,
for theirs is the kingdom of heaven.
(Matthew 5:10–12)

LAST BUT NOT LEAST

This last beatitude might have come as a bit of a shock to Jesus'
original audience. Before we look at its meaning, let's consider it
in the context of the whole list of beatitudes:

Blessed are the poor in spirit,
　　for theirs is the kingdom of heaven.
Blessed are those who mourn,
　　for they will be comforted.
Blessed are the meek,
　　for they will inherit the earth.
Blessed are those who hunger and thirst for righteousness,
　　for they will be filled.
Blessed are the merciful,
　　for they will be shown mercy.
Blessed are the pure in heart,
　　for they will see God.

Blessed are the peacemakers,
> for they will be called sons of God.

Blessed are those who are persecuted because of righteousness,
> for theirs is the kingdom of heaven.

(Blessed are you when people insult you, persecute you and falsely say all kinds of evil against you because of me. Rejoice and be glad, because great is your reward in heaven, for in the same way they persecuted the prophets who were before you.)

It may be hard to avoid a sense of perplexity or even disillusionment as you read the last beatitude. After all, we've had a long climb up the mountain and we feel we deserve a great view from the summit. However, instead of a wonderful pay-off, we get the cold and unnerving promise that being blessed will involve persecution. What a surprising conclusion! It's an anti-climax that seems to prime us for trouble ahead. Here, perhaps not for the first time, you may find yourself feeling puzzled and even irritated by the apparent perversity of Jesus' words.

Although Jesus' words appear to fly in the face of common sense, they in fact embody great wisdom. This statement is unlike the many modern-day proverbs, which go along the lines of: 'Things will get worse before they get better', 'Well, it's all swings and roundabouts' or 'You win some, you lose some.' I suspect that in most cases these are said in order to reassure people that we really have heard their story – we use them as comforting phrases after some awful anecdote draws to a close. Like other platitudes, these phrases say nothing new; they create no ripples in the pools of our minds. I mention this because whatever else they are, the Beatitudes are not platitudes. In fact, they are the very opposite. While platitudes seek to soothe and reduce the likelihood of any response, the Beatitudes are intended to challenge, provoke and disturb. I have no idea what the Aramaic is for 'You what?' or

'Eh?' but I'm fairly sure that Jesus' original hearers would have shown their astonishment with some similar expression. After all, they knew better than we do what persecution really means. They didn't have to imagine what stoning and crucifixion did to you.

There is actually some evidence that Jesus' original listeners did find this statement a bit much to stomach. At the end of this beatitude alone, Jesus adds a further comment to reinforce what he has said. So this eighth beatitude is immediately followed by an expansion of what it means: 'Blessed are you when people insult you, persecute you, and falsely say all kinds of evil against you because of me. Rejoice and be glad, because great is your reward in heaven, for in the same way they persecuted the prophets who were before you' (Matthew 5:11–12). Some people see this as a ninth beatitude, but it's hard to see how it differs in any significant way from the eighth. In any case, the fact that both the first and eighth beatitudes have the same blessing – that of receiving the kingdom of heaven – is a pretty sure sign that, like matching bookends, they are the beginning and the end of the Beatitudes. It seems far more sensible to see verses 11 and 12 as a comment expanding and developing the original blessing relating to this eighth beatitude. On this basis, I have taken the liberty of slightly modifying the translation by putting the addition of verses 11 and 12 in brackets because this makes it clear that it is a reinforcement of the central idea.

Whatever your own initial reaction to the message of this beatitude, can I assure that it does fit into the list and it makes a very grand finale. We started the Beatitudes in the depths of consciousness, with the twin ideas of being poor in spirit and mourning over our own sinfulness. These are like the roots that anchor the great tree of blessing. In the next two beatitudes, we were taught about the trunk of that mighty tree, which consists of two principles of growth: the meekness that leads to teachability and the desire for righteousness, which should drive us upwards. After this we saw two great branches, the twin priorities of mercy towards others and purity of heart for ourselves. In the seventh beatitude, we learned about the fruit of the tree of blessing: the bringing of peace to both humankind and our world. Now, finally, we learn how that fruit will be received.

In the eighth beatitude, Jesus shows again that He cannot gloss over the truth. He makes no attempt to hide the reality of life as a Christian. Christians have all too frequently treated the Beatitudes in such a 'religious' or 'spiritual' way that the idea of being 'persecuted' has acquired a halo of sanctification which not only makes it respectable, but harmless and removed from everyday life. We use the word 'persecution' to refer to other places and other times, as in 'the persecuted martyrs of the Early Church' or the 'persecuted Christians of Indonesia', putting it into stained-glass language, scented with the faint whiff of incense, so that it becomes non-threatening. But this is unhelpful. We need to 'get real' with the idea of persecution. Persecution is about rejection, pain, tears, blood and fear – and these things are experienced by Christians every day, even at this very moment while you are reading this book.

However unpleasant this may seem, it is vital that we consider persecution because – as Jesus is explaining – this is the *fruit* of the tree which represents a Christian lifestyle. It is something we certainly need to learn more about and face up to if we are truly to accept the message of the gospel and become blessed and happy.

THE TRIGGER FOR PERSECUTION: RIGHTEOUSNESS

So what causes Christian persecution? It is quite simply the *righteousness* which Jesus brings, both through His teachings and also through His death on the cross. (It is not for nothing that He is described as a 'righteous one' in Acts 3:14.) This righteousness, which we may be honoured to share through belief in Jesus, has a dramatic impact on the broken world it encounters. It is as if cold water is thrown onto a fire. There is inevitably a loud reaction because two elements, which are profoundly dissimilar, are suddenly brought into contact with each other. The blunt truth that Jesus teaches here is that if we do seek to live out righteousness then we'll be challenged to the core. Persecution is inevitable. We may make great efforts to be meek, merciful, pure in heart and peacemaking but our efforts will not be greeted with bouquets and applause; instead we're bound to get boos and thrown bricks! Other people will dislike us when God blesses us. Instead of inviting us, along with other celebrities, to TV interviews and special events, people are likely to actively try and make our lives miserable. Jesus, the great revolutionary, takes the idea of worldly success and overturns it.

In a culture with very little commitment to moral standards, someone who is trying to live out righteousness is going to provoke a reaction. Just as our bodies unleash defence mechanisms when a foreign object such as a virus enters our bloodstream, so the world also reacts to the presence of an active and living Christianity. That aggressive defensive reaction manifests in persecution.

Many people find something very uncomfortable about righteousness. Those who have no interest in holiness find a concern about righteousness to be offensive. The whole idea makes them feel morally under-dressed, as if they had been caught wearing dirty jeans at a smart party. When you don't really care much about morality, it's fairly easy to convince yourself that you're really not too bad. That belief is impossible to maintain when someone comes along with high moral standards and makes an effort to keep them. When people's *immorality* is inadvertently exposed by *morality*, persecution is almost inevitable.

Consider a few very practical examples. Think of an accountant in a firm who uncovers unethical practices, and realises he has no choice but to find another job. Think what might happen when a sales rep is asked to promote a product which she knows is unethical. How will a shop manager get on when he's told that he must work most Sundays, meaning that his church commitment will be hopelessly compromised? Here, although the issues may be complex, the lines of righteousness, and potential persecution, are clearly drawn.

In other cases, reasons for persecution are somewhat more subtle. To use an old phrase, the problem is simply that Christians 'dance to a different tune'. Being a Christian means putting your ultimate allegiance with Christ. This causes enormous problems in situations where organisations require a strong allegiance. A classic historical case is, once more, to be found in the Roman Empire. The expanding Empire found itself needing to somehow hold together a vast range of diverse peoples. It soon became clear that one of the simplest ways of keeping everybody united was to encourage universal commitment to the Emperor. The nature of the required devotion gradually increased so while only some people were worshipping Caesar by the end of the first century, only a century later his worship had become compulsory. Once a year or so, all citizens had to make an offering to the Emperor and say, 'Caesar is Lord.' Since this was more an act of political allegiance than religious worship, it seems that most Romans shrugged their shoulders, burnt some incense, repeated the words and then went about their everyday business, which may or may not have included worshipping whatever gods they fancied. Christians, however, felt they could not compromise their faith with this allegiance and worship of Caesar, so they fell foul of the authorities. Because the Roman Empire could not tolerate such acts of open disloyalty, early Christians were soon brutally persecuted.

The same happens today, although not quite in the same way, of course. The persecution of Christians often occurs not so much because others are opposed to what they believe in, but simply because Christians refuse to toe the party line. In the interests of creating 'corporate unity', 'mutual bonding' or 'harmonious relationships', followers of Christ find themselves being discriminated against. In situations as diverse as the Roman Empire, Hitler's Germany and modern multinational corporations, Christians have found themselves having to take a stand against what is wrong.

Note that when Jesus says we will be persecuted like prophets who came before us, He is putting us in the same class as the ancient prophets. What an honour! After all, these people were persecuted because of their commitment to God. By saying that we will be persecuted 'because of Him', Jesus is quietly and subtly making a statement that only makes sense if applied to God and appropriating it to Himself. It is an action that would frankly be blasphemous if Jesus were not, in fact, God made flesh.

RIGHTEOUSNESS CAN BE FOUND IN CHRIST ALONE

Because there is a temptation to see the Beatitudes as moral statements made by someone who was no more than one of this world's many good teachers, it is worth lingering over the point that Jesus was God. You sometimes meet people (particularly from the Islamic community or from the New Age community) who dismiss any idea that Christ is more than a prophet or a great teacher. These people justify their interpretation by saying, 'Nowhere in the Gospels does Jesus say "I am God"!' Actually, it is not hard to see several possible reasons why Jesus did not utter those exact words. One reason is that it is actually very misleading. After all, if Jesus had said, 'I am God,' that could easily have been taken as a claim that He was all that God was. To my knowledge no Christian church has ever held that view. The idea that God is Trinity (Father, Son and Spirit) does not lend itself to being summed up in a single, snappy three-word claim. Things are more complex than that. A second possible reason why Jesus was restrained in

His claims to be God is that much of His teaching was characterised by subtlety (out of choice) and secrecy (out of necessity). In most of His teaching Jesus seems to have been trying to seek out those people who wanted to know the truth while at the same time ensuring that He would not be prematurely executed for blasphemy.

If Jesus was not as blunt and overt in His claims to be God as we might like, we cannot escape the fact that in many different ways Jesus did claim to have an identity with God. Again and again in His teachings, His healings and His miracles, Jesus either said or did what only Yahweh, the Lord and God of the Old Testament, could say and do. On almost every page of the Gospels we find Jesus, without embarrassment, apology or publicity, making claims to be one with God. In dozens of ways, some obvious but many not, He showed He could be identified with God and that He deserved the right to be worshipped. When, for instance, towards the end of John's Gospel, Thomas says to Jesus, 'My Lord and my God' (John 20:28) this is merely the recognition of the validity of claims that Jesus has been making throughout His ministry. We must remember how staggering it was at this time for someone to call Jesus 'Lord' and 'God'. People would not even utter the name Yahweh (God) on their lips. If they wrote 'YHWH' on the ground, they would wash their hands first. And here the followers of Jesus were calling Jesus God. This was radical for the staunchly monotheistic world of Judaism. Those who had followed Jesus and who thought deeply about what He said, did indeed recognise that He was someone who was greater than any prophet. Jesus was nothing short of God on earth. No wonder they could not keep quiet about the news that the Messiah had indeed come to earth. There are many today who have come to the same conclusion.

Now I mention this here not simply to make a point about Jesus' identity but to emphasise that righteousness can only be found in Jesus. Some people remain under the illusion that they can somehow achieve the righteousness the Bible demands by themselves. 'Oh I believe in God,' they say, 'and right and wrong, but I don't agree with you on all this emphasis about Jesus. I don't need him.' All I can say is that throughout the New Testament, God's righteousness is inextricably linked with Jesus. Indeed, it is never linked with anything else – least of all 'good behaviour', which the Bible recognises we are all unhappily incapable of achieving. Righteousness (and, with it, blessing and happiness) flows only from one channel: Christ.

If I had to summarise the teaching of the New Testament and righteousness simply I would say this: 'We must accept God's righteousness in Jesus and we must reflect God's right-eousness in Jesus.' The two aspects are part of a single whole. We become Christ's by choosing to accept Him but that is not the end of the story; once that commitment is made we need to live in such a way as to show that we reflect His nature. As I said in Chapter 4, the pursuit of righteousness begins with a concern about how we live and from there spreads out to a concern about the way in which the whole world lives.

To accept Christ's righteousness is to accept a change of owner-ship and identity. This decision has serious ramifications for our lives. Let me give one of many possible illustrations. Imagine some shabby and struggling corner shop on the point of imminent closure through debts, which is suddenly taken over by a larger chain of rather classy stores. Money is injected into the shop, there is new paintwork, new stock and a new logo: all is changed. With the upgrades and investments comes the expectation that the shop will reflect its new owners. It is now part of something much grander and there is no intention that it should sink back to its former shabby state. So it is with our lives: God rescues us, adopts us into His family and then effectively says: 'You are one of my children now! Live out your new identity as my son or daughter.'

To help us with this task He also gives us Christ's power through the Holy Spirit. In the New Testament the Holy Spirit is given a Greek word *parakletos* (John 14:16; 15:26; 16:7). This word is hard to translate, but most English versions settle (rather unsatisfactorily) for 'comforter' or 'counsellor'. The word really means 'one who stands alongside to assist' and the idea is of a helper or someone who will support us. So it is that our attempt to live out a Jesus-like righteousness does not have to be undertaken in our own strength. We have God's own helper, the Holy Spirit, to assist us.

THE NATURE OF PERSECUTION

What does it look like to be persecuted today? In considering what forms persecution takes and why it occurs, we will also need to sort out right and wrong reasons for being persecuted.

What is persecution?

It's easy to set up a misleading caricature of persecution. In my experience, we tend to think of two main images. One is what we might call the 'classical version': here, we imagine that in some sun-baked amphitheatre noble Christian men and women are thrown to the lions in front of some bloated, purple-clad emperor and a brutish mob. Or we may choose the 'East European version' where in chill damp cells hard-faced men in drab military uniform kick handcuffed prisoners. The reality is that both images are misguided; persecution is more extensive and more varied than either of these caricatures suggests. Jesus himself makes this clear when He broadens the definition of what it means to be persecuted. He says: 'Blessed are you when people insult you, persecute you and falsely say all kinds of evil against you because of me.' In other words, although being slandered and insulted is pretty minor compared to being torn apart by wild animals, it is still part and parcel of persecution – so we need to consider this alongside any more apparently 'extreme' forms of physical persecution.

Persecution can be divided into three categories: the incidental, the trivial and the bitter.

'Incidental' persecution

This kind of persecution might involve losing a productivity bonus because you're too honest to fiddle the figures like everybody else. Or it might mean missing out on promotion because you're giving too much time to charitable work or because you choose not to get roaring drunk with everybody else on a regular basis. It may mean ending up with the desk, computer or task that no one else wants simply because your boss knows that *you* won't have a shouting fit about it. It might mean not getting the credit for work you've done yourself, and even being criticised or sidelined by the person who takes credit instead.

This sort of incidental persecution happens not just to individuals but also to organisations. Christian organisations may end up having to opt out of potentially advantageous agreements with potential partners because it would involve compromise with principles they hold dear.

Whether it's experienced by individuals or organisations, this kind of persecution is clearly unpleasant, not only because of its immediate financial or practical effects but also because of its undermining and demoralising effect. Suddenly, instead of achieving something – a business deal, an award for sport, or a good review – you find the world either ignoring you or condemning you. In worldly terms, you have 'failed'. In some ways, this is worse than being thrown into jail for your faith because at least that way you get praise or respect. But to have to come to terms with having the title 'failure' hanging around your neck is hard, and certainly doesn't feel remotely heroic.

'Trivial' persecution

This kind of persecution can take many forms. It may involve being cold-shouldered at the coffee bar, not being invited to the neighbours' party, or being given the worst class to teach. It might mean being given the worst shifts at work, becoming the focus of sly digs at a staff meeting or being picked on for early retirement. It may be so incredibly subtle that it remains almost unnoticed until the 'victim' perceives that he or she is not part of that vital inner circle that all organisations have, where the really important decisions are made.

This sort of trivial persecution also occurs at the corporate level. For example, a Christian fellowship may be excluded from meeting on company premises, another similar venture may be excluded from public funding and a church may have to jump through extra hoops for planning permission. This kind of persecution frequently occurs to family or friends of the 'persecuted'. Many Christians find it particularly hurtful the way their children, for example, are persecuted simply because of their own lifestyle. Where is the justice in that?

Although some people learn to live with this trivial persecution, many find it draining and depressing. The reality is that most of us prefer to be liked. Speaking as something of an outsider to British culture, I find the famous British tendency towards 'tolerance' absolutely fascinating. If you come up with some outrageous argument that you know your hearer will disagree with, in all likelihood all he or she will do is hesitate, look unhappy and then say slowly, 'Well, I see your point of view' or 'Hmm, I know where you're coming from.' Brits, like many other human beings on the planet, actively dislike disagreement and avoid it wherever possible. Although this gives rise to a splendidly open and diverse society in which differences of opinion and lifestyle can be permitted, this extraordinary aversion to causing trouble can pressure us to into supporting things that we know are wrong.

I think this sort of trivial persecution is growing in the West. As countries like Britain move out of their nominally Christian status to a post-Christian and even pagan mood, this sort of persecution is becoming increasingly acceptable. Like clouds gathering before a thunderstorm, accusations are beginning to accumulate. Christians are increasingly perceived as 'anti-gay', as being 'opposed to women's rights', as 'wanting to get rid of science', as being 'against medical progress', and so on. However much you try to counter such arguments, the allegations continue. Perhaps the most irritating one is the insinuation that all Christians are naïve, stupid or simplistic. Given the appalling 'dumbing down' present in contemporary culture this one in particular seems grotesquely unfair. It is not thanks to Christians that we have the tabloid press, the mind-numbing idiocy of reality TV or political arguments which have to be reduced to a single soundbite. Yet the allegations persist and some of the mud will stick.

It's interesting that such attacks on Christianity seem to have increased since 9/11. One interpretation for this is that the attacks are being made by those who really would like to attack Islam but dare not. (After all, *that* might be construed as racism.) Christianity seems to be an easier target, especially since we're the ones who apparently 'turn the other cheek'. Of course, this is hardly fair, but then if persecution were fair it wouldn't be persecution. Incidentally, as a minister I find this mood of contempt for Christianity very frustrating. One of the dangerous things about being scornful of something is that it automatically prevents any serious discussion of the topic at issue. Being scornful of something involves inoculating yourself against the possibility that you may be wrong. Abuse becomes a substitute for engagement on any level.

'Bitter' persecution

The sort of apparently 'trivial' dislike for Christianity and Christians we have just discussed can easily slide into a far more serious type of persecution, which we shall call 'bitter'. It is a sad reflection on human nature that we like to have enemies. Christians, by virtue of being distinct and standing up for such unpopular things as truth, honesty and decency, are very vulnerable to becoming someone else's enemy. There is a common pattern to much persecution of Christians that goes back to the first bitter persecution which occurred under the Emperor Nero. In AD 64, a catastrophic fire swept through Rome and rumours spread among the survivors that Emperor Nero, who was riding low in the popularity polls, had started it himself. The historian Tacitus tells us that the Emperor, finding this rumour uncomfortably persistent and threatening, decided to blame the Christians. He instigated a merciless campaign against them and had many of them executed in the cruellest possible ways.

This sort of pattern has recurred ever since. Whether it be an army, an economy or a sports team that has failed, people have always found it useful to make Christians the scapegoat. (Traditionally, the prime candidates for blame were Jews, but these days the much larger, more visible and more widespread Christian community seems to be an easier target.) In many countries there have been unpleasant cases where Christian members of the middle class have found themselves the victims of accusations. That way you can kill two birds with one stone; throw the Christians to the lions (or the current equivalent) and seize their property and assets too.

It is a sad fact that the current level of persecution against

Christians world-wide is astonishingly high. There are many atheist, Hindu or Islamic regimes and cultures that have allowed, or even encouraged, the punishment or imprisonment of Christians. The website of Christian Solidarity Worldwide, a Christian human rights non-governmental organisation which specialises in religious freedom, works on behalf of those persecuted for their Christian beliefs and promotes religious liberty for all, highlights news stories that bring home this reality. Two Christian girls of ten and thirteen were recently abducted in Pakistan while on a trip to visit their uncle, they were forced to convert to Islam and one of them was made to marry her abductor. A Sri-Lankan pastor was attacked by three men while walking home from a church meeting. Chinese house church leaders have been detained by police for months on end. Cuban security agents entered a church by force and beat eighteen human rights activists attending a mass there. The list goes on.

And even martyrdom still occurs embarrassingly close to home. There are many cultures, some of which are now well represented in most Western countries, where changing your religion is such a blow to the honour of the family that only the 'guilty' person's death can remove the shame. It is impossible to know how many martyrs for Christianity there have been among converts in Western countries in the last thirty years, but people who have tried to track this suspect the figures run into the hundreds, if not thousands.

WHEN IS PERSECUTION NOT 'BLESSED'?

Jesus is noticeably specific that His followers will be blessed when they suffer for the sake of righteousness. Of course, there are other, extremely non-Christian reasons why people experience the types of persecution we've discussed, but these will not bring the blessing about which Jesus is speaking. Perhaps there are four situations that we should watch out for, which are not 'persecution for righteousness'.

When it's because of everyday troubles

First, Jesus excludes troubles which are simply the product of everyday life. We may suffer sickness, be made redundant, have our home broken into, or get old. These things are, sadly, part of the package of being human. They normally have nothing at all to do with righteousness. So if you break a leg skiing, please don't feel you can claim any sort of moral compensation by assuming it's an affirmation of your righteousness. It may simply be because you're a bad skier or slipped on a bit of unfortunately situated ice.

When it's for doing the wrong thing

If we simply do something wrong, the hassle or the flak we experience afterwards also can't be put down to righteousness. This ought to be so obvious it shouldn't need to be said, but it's easy to misread biblical texts and some people seem to see this passage as saying simply 'blessed are those who are persecuted'. *Sorry!* Nowhere in the Bible does Jesus (or anyone else) ever suggest that suffering is praiseworthy or glorious in itself. Getting a parking ticket or a speeding fine is not persecution, it's probably justice in action.

The expansion of this beatitude actually makes this totally obvious. Jesus says: 'Blessed are you when people insult you, persecute you and *falsely* say all kinds of evil against you.' There is no blessing for those who are justifiably accused of evil misdeeds. In the first of his letters the apostle Peter makes the same point: 'If you are insulted because of the name of Christ, you are blessed, for the Spirit of glory and of God rests on you. If you suffer, it should not be as a murderer or thief or any other kind of criminal, or even as a meddler. However, if you suffer as a Christian, do not be ashamed, but praise God that you bear that name' (1 Peter 4:14–16).

When it's for being horrible

Some people, including Christians, bring persecution upon themselves through their own personalities. There are those who seem to aspire to be 'God's Rottweiler', who delight in mercilessly savaging anyone who doesn't fit with their ideals. There are also people who, in the name of the gospel, leap into any debate regardless of whether or not they know anything about the subject. There was a recent case of a biology professor who was so aggressively and naïvely attacked by a creationist at a dinner party, that the following day, still reeling from the encounter, he took the step of faith he had been avoiding for years and openly declared that he was an atheist. It is vital to grasp that the persecution Jesus refers to here is solely for righteousness, not recklessness.

When we're masochists

Finally, there are some people around who actually seem to *want* to be persecuted. Although I have no understanding of the mindset involved, this certainly does happen. It's a sort of spiritual masochism, a perverse delight in suffering. This, along with the other types of 'unblessed' persecution we've considered, should never be sought out for its own sake. As far as possible we should aim to live at peace with all people, as we're instructed to do in Romans 12:18: 'If it is possible, as far as it depends on you, live at peace with everyone.'

WHAT CAUSES PERSECUTION?

Having given an overview earlier in this chapter of why Christians are vulnerable to persecution, it's now also useful to consider other things which might specifically trigger persecution in a modern Christian's life.

Dishonesty

Dishonesty often involves money or personal advantage in one sense or another. If you discover your friends are involved in a tax or expenses fiddle, you have three choices: to join in, to expose what they're doing and resign if necessary, or to ignore your colleagues' lack of honesty. If we care about righteousness, our only real option is to expose any lack of honesty and aim to put this situation right, or to resign and go elsewhere. Obviously, we can't join in and we can hardly feign ignorance either, especially since people are usually strangely open and boastful about dishonest practices. Of course, standing up for what is right in a situation like this is not likely to be a popular course of action.

Corruption

Some cases of corruption may be quite spectacular. Rumour has it, for example, that contracts are frequently negotiated with countries where there is no investigative press. Other cases of corruption may be more subtle, involving the more modest wining and dining of people in a position to do something for us or our company. There are also job advertisements which say 'applications are invited for . . .' but where, in reality, the chosen man or woman is already known well before the interview. Here, again, we may have to make our voice heard, and when we do, we had better be prepared for trouble.

Abuses of human rights

Cases of human rights abuse can be very serious, for example where asylum seekers or economic migrants are treated as little more than slaves. Other cases may involve one group of people treating another group less fairly than others. Friends who have worked in the Middle East have told me appalling stories of how maids from another country are treated. I am not sure treatment of 'economic migrants' in countries such as Britain is much better. Slavery may have been formally abolished but, in reality, something very similar persists even into the twenty-first century.

Lack of integrity

Instances involving a lack of integrity occur increasingly in a world where image counts for more than reality. In some cases the image of a person or place is literally manipulated, with facial or scenic blemishes digitally erased. In other cases, reality is sidelined altogether as a kind of illusion is built up, perhaps for the sake of advertising or publicity. In cases such as these we may have no option but to burst the bubble of illusion and insist that reality be revealed. Like the little boy in Hans Christian Andersen's story, we may have to point out that, for all his posturing, the Emperor's new clothes really are just an illusion. Although that particular tale is obviously rather a naïve one, with a nondescript and inoffensive ending, in real life the Emperor would probably pause for a moment, whisper a quick order to his aides and the boy would quietly be beheaded down a side street. After all, as Jesus implied in this beatitude, persecution usually follows any instance of righteousness.

Poor quality control

One of the oldest tricks for improving profitability is to take a successful product and dilute the key ingredient. Whether it results in a less meaty sausage or a more watery paint, the temptation to cut corners is widespread. Here too, someone may need to blow the whistle, and that someone is not going to be popular.

All these areas are examples of things which may cause persecution, but there are doubtless many others which could be added to the list. The point is that it is impossible to live as one of God's children in this world without a backlash, despite popular opinion to the contrary.

REASONS TO BE CHEERFUL

If this all seems rather depressing, let us at least reassure ourselves that any persecution we experience is seen as part of the 'Grand Plan' throughout the New Testament. There are a number of good reasons to be cheerful about the prospect (or memory) of persecution.

It's a sign we've set out on the right path

Persecution for righteousness authenticates what we are. If you remember anything from your school chemistry lessons you will know that there are various chemical tests which involve testing one substance with another and seeing if a reaction ensues. Persecution is the way the world reacts when it comes into contact with God's righteousness. It is a reaction that demonstrates the authenticity of those who are Christian. In other words, righteousness is the cutting edge of our life, the point where any conflict between our faith and society will be felt. After all, the

Christian life is not simply about declaring that we have accepted Jesus, it means following Him right to the end. Jesus was brutally persecuted until His final blow on the cross. As He stated in the Gospel of John, what happens to the master must also happen to His servants: 'Remember the words I spoke to you: "No servant is greater than his master." If they persecuted me, they will persecute you also' (John 15:20).

It's a sign our faith is taking root

If we are persecuted, it is certainly a sign that we are persevering with our Christian faith. Life is full of beginnings but continuations and good endings are rare. I'm sure you can think of many cases, both sad and serious: those New Year's resolutions that were quickly forgotten; that 12 CD set of *Learn Italian* that never got used; that copy of *War and Peace* with the faded bookmark between pages six and seven; those neatly folded clothes we bought when we went on a diet; the dust-covered cans of paint in the garage that we bought for repainting a room; those broken marriages where both parties said 'till death us do part'.

Jesus was clearly aware of people's tendency to abandon new fads. On several occasions, He is cautious about individuals who decide to follow Him, and in the parable of the sower (Matthew 13:1–23; Mark 4:1–20; Luke 8:4–15) He suggests how few of us will reach the finishing line. In this parable you may recall that very little of the seed which was sown by the farmer yielded any crop. In fact, out of all the seed sown, Jesus says that some fell on a hard path, some sprouted up quickly but soon died in the heat of the sun, yet more was overcome by weeds and only some actually took root and grew successfully. Jesus' intention was clearly not to attract passers-by, with shallow enthusiasm, but people who were ready to put down roots and make a long-term, serious commitment.

This makes sense when we consider that unless we follow Jesus right to the end, our efforts will be in vain. We must continue to the finishing line, even in the face of difficulties and opposition so severe that they threaten our lives. This may seem brutally realistic, but it is at least clear! Jesus says it is not enough to merely accept Him; we must follow Him faithfully to the end. Being persecuted for the sake of righteousness is certainly an excellent sign we're continuing along the right road!

Jesus said we should be glad

Surprisingly, perhaps, Jesus clearly implies that people who are persecuted because of righteousness are to be congratulated. Consider Jesus' amplification of this eighth beatitude. 'Rejoice and be glad,' He says, 'because great is your reward in heaven . . .' So after – or even *during* – the grimness of any persecution, it's time to rejoice. Perhaps the Holy Spirit will help us out here because, as you will no doubt remember, one of His gifts is also joy.

As we mentioned earlier, we should also be glad that we are part of the long and noble line of persecuted people. The persecuted are part of a lineage that is noble by virtue of the fact that God's people are victimised for His truth. In the Old Testament the list of people who were persecuted and godly was very impressive, and includes people such as Joseph, Jeremiah, Elijah and Daniel (see Hebrews 11:36–38). In fact, it is quite rare to find a godly person in the Bible who was not persecuted. Jesus says, in effect, to the persecuted: 'Look at those people and celebrate: you are up there *with* them!'

Jesus cares about us when we're persecuted

As Lord of His people, Jesus is concerned about every detail of their fate. One of the most bizarre incidents in British history is what became known as the 'War of Jenkins' Ear'. In 1739, England went to war over the mistreatment of English seamen, notably Captain Robert Jenkins, who claimed Spanish coast guards had cut off his ear. Jenkins exhibited what was left of the ear in the House of Commons and the result was that the outraged government declared war on Spain. The reality seems to be that the English wanted a war, and Jenkins' misfortune was a convenient excuse to start one. Nevertheless, it's a good story to illustrate how rulers can be concerned about the slightest persecution of their subjects. Whether or not such compassionate rulers exist in our 'broken' world, we can be sure that Jesus is a ruler capable of care over every last detail. He cares passionately about His people because they are His, they belong to His kingdom and those who mistreat them must answer to Him. If you're being persecuted for righteousness be comforted by the knowledge that the King of kings notices every time. Since God is a just God, we should be reassured by this truth.

Jesus will limit any persecution we experience

Here we touch on a great mystery, which I won't attempt to try and answer now. Why does God allow evil to occur, even though He is good and just? The Bible does at least tell us that although God is neither evil nor responsible for evil, He does oversee the working of evil and limit its effects. (We learn this from the book of Job.) In other words, nothing happens to us except with God's say-so. Evil may appear to know no limits but it is in fact strictly restrained. The persecuted must realise that although appearances may suggest otherwise, God remains King and is in charge over all. Difficult to understand, no doubt, but this too is certainly a 'reason to be cheerful'.

Jesus will make sure persecution is used for our own good

Somehow, God allows suffering to occur for His people's good. Although it might be difficult for us to understand how this happens in specific situations, we can perhaps imagine that pain and suffering are capable of producing a refining effect that makes everything worthwhile. Paul explains, 'We rejoice in the hope of the glory of God. Not only so, but we also rejoice in our sufferings, because we know that suffering produces perseverance; perseverance, character; and character, hope' (Romans 5:2–4). In God's hands suffering refines us, and prunes away those things that distract and threaten our identity.

Jesus will reward us for being persecuted

One reason why persecution seems so problematic and upsetting is that we do not see the full story. We are only able to see what is happening in this world; we see the problems, but not the future rewards. We can certainly be reassured, though, that the King will compensate anybody who suffers for the sake of His kingdom. One of the few palaces in Britain, the splendid Blenheim Palace near Oxford, was constructed to be a gift from a grateful monarch to John Churchill, the 1st Duke of Marlborough. This gift was intended to express the king's thanks for John Churchill's military triumphs on the continent in the first decade of the eighteenth century. The successful combatant was given a magnificent reward. We may take it that a similar policy works in the spiritual realm. The King will reward and recompense all those who have served Him and suffered for Him. And I might venture to guess that nobody is going to complain about the rate of exchange between the blows we suffer in this world and the blessings we're given in the next. The eternal kingdom may seem a remote and distant concept, yet for those who suffer for the King, the very thought of it is a source of rich and abundant blessing.

The prize is worth it

We need to be aware that we're going to get more than a palace! Now when we turn to look at exactly what Jesus promises to those who are persecuted for righteousness we get a surprise: it's nothing less than the kingdom of heaven! This is exactly the same kingdom that the poor in spirit received in the first beatitude.

We must remember that the kingdom of heaven is the sum of all God's riches, and hidden within it are blessings of unlimited peace, joy, security and wealth. To receive the kingdom is to receive everything that we could ever want for as long as we can ever imagine. When the kingdom of heaven comes in all its glory there will be no good thing missing from within it. (The opposite is sadly true: outside the eternal kingdom there will be nothing good present.)

Now I talked a lot about the kingdom of heaven in Chapter 1 and do not propose to repeat myself here, but there are aspects of it which we need to think about afresh, particularly in the context of this beatitude. This is because, as I said earlier, one of the dangers we face when thinking about the kingdom is that we think of it in terms of geography or politics. It's far safer to think of it in terms of a relationship. In other words, we may be better off focusing on the King as a person, rather than the kingdom as a place. So we become a member of the kingdom offering our allegiance to the King. In the context of persecution, this is extremely helpful and provides much comfort.

Jesus said this would happen

Finally, we can be reassured by the fact that Jesus predicted persecution all along. In Luke's Gospel, after speaking about His return, Jesus gives us a solemn warning and a great promise:

> But before all this they will lay hands on you and persecute you. They will deliver you to synagogues and prisons, and you will be brought before kings and governors, and all on account of my name. This will result in your being witnesses to them ... You will be betrayed even by parents, brothers, relatives and friends, and they will put some of you to death. All men will hate you because of me. But not a hair of your head will perish. By standing firm you will gain life. (Luke 21:12–14, 16–19)

Here He was saying that anybody who follows Him will be persecuted in the short term, but will inherit the kingdom and gain eternal life in the long run, as was His grand plan all along.

REASONS TO BE WARY

After so much positivity on the subject of persecution, we must unfortunately end this chapter with some provocative questions.

Why do Christians in the West so rarely get persecuted?

Sometimes I wonder if, in the West, we ought to be more worried by the problem of prosperity than the problem of persecution. If the hallmark of the righteous is persecution, what does the fact that we are not persecuted say about us? Has our righteousness become so diluted that we are not sufficiently different to provoke the world into a reaction? If you know anything of biology or ecology, you will know that there are two strategies to stop yourself being eaten. One is to acquire teeth and armour, so as to make yourself unpalatable. The other is to adopt a camouflage or change your habits so that predators don't notice you. Have we already gone down that path? Have we become part of the fabric of the world instead of being distinctive from it?

Think for a moment about the alternative to persecution – to permanently agree with whatever other people say. It means always compromising, being infinitely flexible, and having the moral fibre of a jellyfish. You may survive, but that is all you're likely to do. Living like this, how could you ever be happy or fulfilled?

A friend told me how he took up a new job and found himself regularly working with a senior figure in the organisation. My friend was agreeably flattered when, on the first day, his colleague agreed with everything that he said. Then, as the days passed by and the man continued to agree with everything he said, my friend gradually lost any respect he had once had for this senior manager. He realised that his colleague's words had no real value.

If you want to be satisfied and fulfilled, you have no alternative but to stick up for what you believe. If you don't, however rich your external blessings may be, you'll lose everything that really counts. If you try to sacrifice integrity for the sake of happiness, you'll find you lose all chance of happiness.

We must also be careful about bending our principles. This is perhaps the most dangerous approach of all, because the truth of the matter is that principles are often not so much suddenly broken as gently bent out of shape. Slowly, imperceptibly, without us realising what has happened, we begin to merge with the world's way of doing things.

Why do we so often give up?

Despite all manner of warnings and resolutions, many people still take a look at Jesus and His teaching and say, 'Wonderful! Just what I've been looking for. Count me in!' Then, a month or so later, they're conspicuous by their absence. The pattern of the past has not changed. Many start, few finish and in most cases the reason for people's failure to persevere is that they met opposition or difficulties, and gave up. They didn't face up to the persecution! Why is this such a perennial problem?

It is a traditional and a useful view to see human behaviour as being driven by the head, the heart and the will. The *heart* is the centre of the emotions, the home of the desires and the dreams. Notoriously, the heart is prone to great and almost irresistible surges of energy, which often prove to be temporary. The *head* is the area of intellectual choice. Here we weigh up the pros and cons, consider matters carefully, and then make our reasoned preference. The *will* drives both decision and determination. The will may consider both the desires of the heart and the judgements of the head, and can overrule both.

Consider how all three operate in the case of a marriage. A man and woman fall in love and, driven by heart, head and will, they get married. All is wonderful and the sun shines on the relationship. But as the years pass, illness descends on one partner. After a long and wearying period, the other partner realises there is the possibility of a new romance with someone else. That which would have been impossible to even consider at the start of the marriage now becomes an attractive and tantalising prospect. The heart says, 'I want a new relationship' and the head murmurs agreement, saying: 'After all, this may be your last chance of happiness.' The will, though, clings on to that promise made long ago, and resists.

Something like this goes on in the Christian life. We come to faith, possibly for a mixture of reasons of head and heart, and then press on. But, sooner or later, troubles dog our path and the way becomes very difficult. Our hearts find little joy to motivate us onwards; our head tells us that it is all fantasy. Yet our will drives us on and we continue, sometimes in darkness, and often against opposition. Generally without warning, the clouds vanish, the sun shines and the road of following Jesus becomes easier once more. Whether we travel in sunlight or shadow, we have to tell ourselves that we must follow Jesus to the end of our days on earth.

Our culture often emphasises the beginning of the Christian life. Indeed, the fact of someone becoming a Christian is extremely exciting. However, we must remember that a conversion is just a beginning; the secret is to finish. Imagine a painter who, amid great publicity, starts painting some enormous canvas. Can you imagine the pressure there would be, as the days and weeks go by, to finish the work? The fear that this process might acquire that most depressing of titles, 'an unfinished work', is something that drives the painter on to complete it. It's the same with the Christian life. We cannot stop and give up without ruining everything. Only finished work counts: we must keep going right to the end.

This principle of the need for persistence is an utterly vital one. Without persistence dreams stay dreams, strategy never becomes more than imaginings and morality becomes little more than pious sentiment. It is not enough to want something, to plan something or even to decide something; we must persevere to completion. We must finish and finish well. Can you imagine the verdict of history on a marathon runner who always started strongly but never completed more than half the course? They would be utterly forgotten. This last beatitude says that we must keep on until the very end.

What if we don't make the grade?

If we don't cross that finishing line, all our efforts will have been wasted.

In Jesus' own words, in case you need reminding, 'Blessed are those who are persecuted because of righteousness, for theirs is the kingdom of heaven.' This is the great capstone of the Beatitudes. It says that it is not enough to give mental assent to the previous seven beatitudes, but they must be lived out through all the days we are given. We must proclaim through laughter and tears. For those who do hold fast to them, there is the richest and greatest comfort. Even in this life there is a deep happiness in trying to follow the Beatitudes, and that happiness is just the faintest fore-taste of the unimaginable and unshakeable happiness that will be ours in the eternal kingdom of heaven.

How to be Happy

In case you would like to read the Beatitudes again, here's a reminder:

Now when he saw the crowds, he went up on a mountainside and sat down. His disciples came to him, and he began to teach them, saying:

Blessed are the poor in spirit,
    for theirs is the kingdom of heaven.
Blessed are those who mourn,
    for they will be comforted.
Blessed are the meek,
    for they will inherit the earth.
Blessed are those who hunger and thirst for righteousness,
    for they will be filled.
Blessed are the merciful,
    for they will be shown mercy.
Blessed are the pure in heart,
    for they will see God.
Blessed are the peacemakers,
    for they will be called sons of God.
Blessed are those who are persecuted because of righteousness,
    for theirs is the kingdom of heaven.

Blessed are you when people insult you, persecute you and falsely say all kinds of evil against you because of me. Rejoice and be glad, because great is your reward in heaven, for in the same way they persecuted the prophets who were before you. (Matthew 5:1–12)

WHAT WERE THEY ALL ABOUT AGAIN?

To get an immediate impression of their meaning, let's turn the Beatitudes on their head. Here are the 'anti-beatitudes'. Instead of 'blessed' let's use the word 'condemned':

The proud in spirit are condemned,
 for theirs is the kingdom of hell.
Those who are careless and proud are condemned,
 for they will never be comforted.
The arrogant are condemned,
 for they will inherit nothing.
Those who hunger and thirst for what is wrong are condemned,
 for they will be always be empty.
The merciless are condemned,
 for they will be shown no mercy.
The devious are condemned,
 for they will never see God.
The troublemakers are condemned,
 for they will be called the children of the Devil.
Those who are honoured because of their wickedness are
 condemned, for theirs is the kingdom of hell.

Now let's review each beatitude, noting the underlying message of each one.

BLESSED ARE THE POOR IN SPIRIT

Jesus says in the first beatitude that people who know they cannot get into heaven by their own strength are blessed, i.e. to be congratulated. The people Jesus includes in this category are those who know they're overdrawn at the bank of heaven, who realise their only hope lies in God's grace and mercy, and whose faith in God is not based on how great they are, but on how gracious He is. Here Jesus congratulates those who humbly come to Him, seeking grace.

It's important to realise that Jesus is not simply talking about a vague acknowledgement of sin, but about a solid awareness that our present balance sheet looks extremely unhealthy. He is, in effect, saying that people who acknowledge their moral bankruptcy are the ones who will be blessed. These people will come into a right relationship with God, become part of the kingdom and serve Him, while He protects and blesses them. When you look at the financial news you probably think, like most people, 'If only I had invested in property or something years ago, I'd be so wealthy.' Yet the wisest decision of all is to invest in the kingdom of God.

BLESSED ARE THOSE WHO MOURN

This beatitude is far more than a message of sympathy and consolation to people who are grieving over earthly events. Instead, it concentrates more on our attitude toward our own lives. To mourn in this context means recognising in our hearts that we have failed God. It means an awareness that we need to repent for what we've done wrong. If the first beatitude is an intellectual acceptance of God's verdict on our lives, the second is the emotional acceptance of our moral failure. Jesus says that people who grieve over what they are will be given comfort. People who mourn now over their spiritual state will be eternally joyful. Indeed, they may know something of that joy in this life. The unhappy will be made happy. This and the first beatitude lay the foundation of what we are meant to be as followers of Jesus.

BLESSED ARE THE MEEK

Here, Jesus is praising people who are modest and humble. Having understood in their heads that they fall short of God's standards and having realised in their hearts how deplorable this is, these people realise that the true basis for life and happiness is dependence on God. The people Jesus is blessing in this beatitude know that they can do nothing without God's power. Faced with life's difficulties and challenges they ask God for guidance and strength. When they're successful, their achievement doesn't go to their heads. They are genuinely able to say, 'God did it all.' They are so modest that they're delighted to see other people triumph and take the glory. God can use these people because they are teachable. Although they would be the first to admit that they deserve nothing, the delightful irony is that God, in His grace, gives them everything.

BLESSED ARE THOSE WHO HUNGER AND THIRST FOR RIGHTEOUSNESS

This beatitude talks about our goals and drives. What do we seek in life? Pleasure? Money? Status? There could be many answers. This is the most important topic of all because it is our ambitions that make or break us. We all know people who suffer from such inadequate motivation that they fail to fulfil their potential.

In the same way, we have heard about people whose motivation is so twisted and inappropriate that it destroys their lives, and sometimes the lives of others.

Jesus says here that the only thing we should long for is right-eousness. We need to seek justice for others and ourselves, and intervene on behalf of the weak and downtrodden. We need to delight in truth, honesty and fairness, while rejecting lies, decep-tion and spin. Indeed, we need to be better than people who are only vaguely interested in righteousness, as if it were something we might vote for in a by-election. We need to have an intense and overpowering desire for righteousness, so that it is our biggest priority in life.

Here, as elsewhere, we see God's enjoyment of irony. Most people hunger and thirst for power, pleasure and possessions, and even when they get them, they're not satisfied. On the other hand, it is people who hunger and thirst for what is right that He satis-fies. The only yearning that will ever be fully met is the yearning for righteousness.

BLESSED ARE THE MERCIFUL

This and the next beatitude offer us two rules for spiritually and relationally healthy living, dealing with our actions and reactions to others. It stipulates that we need to be gentle, generous and gracious. We need to do all that we can to help others. We need to avoid crushing the weak and lift them up instead. At the same time, we need to avoid throwing our weight around. Living in a harsh, cold world, we need to be compassionate and sympathetic towards the suffering. If we behave like this, Jesus says that we will be shown mercy ourselves. Since God's greatest characteristic is mercy it makes sense that He will show us mercy in this way, if we choose to turn to Him.

BLESSED ARE THE PURE IN HEART

While the previous beatitude touched on our motives, this one emphasises the need for our motives to remain pure. The greatest temptation is not that we will suddenly cease to do good, but that we will increasingly begin to do things which are wrong in the name of what is good and right. We must beware of our hearts becoming contaminated or tarnished. This beatitude praises people who really love purity and persist in doing right, despite constant pressure to do wrong things. Their prize is the greatest prize of all: to see God. This means that even in this life they will have a foretaste of what it means to stand in the presence of God. Jesus says that in the next life they will enjoy that privilege forever.

BLESSED ARE THE PEACEMAKERS

This beatitude summarises the way in which God calls His people to embody peace. We are to be a blessing to those around us by carrying out acts of goodness. We also need to bring reconciliation between people and God, between other people, and even between people and God's creation. As far as is possible, we need to put out fires rather than fan them into flame – to bring healing and restoration in difficult situations, rather than aggravate them. We need to work to bring people together, and avoid encouraging bitterness and division. Jesus praises the peacemakers. They are entitled to be God's heirs because they behave in the same way as God.

BLESSED ARE THOSE WHO ARE PERSECUTED BECAUSE OF RIGHTEOUSNESS

Finally, Jesus turns to how those who follow Him and try to live out the Beatitudes will be received. Here He gives the solemn and very realistic warning that people who live out a Christ-like life will know something of the reaction that Jesus received: they will know persecution. Worldly people may say that they approve of righteousness, but when righteousness begins to cost them, they will find it unattractive. Behind Jesus' warning is the encouragement to persist. There is the clear implication that following Jesus should not be a one-off decision, but a lasting struggle against the pressures that distract us, which will continue until the grave. The message is that we need stickability! People who do persist, we are told, will ultimately receive God's riches in heaven.

THE OVERALL MESSAGE

The essential message of the Beatitudes is that our private life is to have a public effect. This message is as relevant to us today as it was when Jesus gave this teaching around 2,000 years ago. His words were not some hotchpotch of ideas put together to entertain a primitive, rural audience, but words of wisdom which have relevance to all people for all times. Nothing that He said is outdated, archaic or irrelevant in our twenty-first-century world. For as long as human beings exist, these teachings provide the clear message that we need to translate our beliefs into our lifestyle.

The notion that we must demonstrate our beliefs and attitudes is emphasised by the fact that, immediately after the Beatitudes, we have the following verses:

> You are the salt of the earth. But if the salt loses its saltiness,
> how can it be made salty again? It is no longer good for
> anything, except to be thrown out and trampled by men.
> You are the light of the world. A city on a hill cannot be hidden.
> Neither do people light a lamp and put it under a bowl. Instead
> they put it on its stand, and it gives light to everyone in the
> house. In the same way, let your light shine before men, that
> they may see your good deeds and praise your Father in heaven.
> (Matthew 5:13–16)

In other words, the test of whether or not we are followers of
Jesus relates not to how often we attend church or how loudly we
praise, but to how productively we live out His teachings in our
daily lives.

Given the cultural history of the Jews and their emphasis on
details of the Law (outlined in the Old Testament, and expanded
in many other rabbinic texts), it is notable that the teaching Jesus
gives does not focus on legal detail. His teachings do not relate
to the clothes we should wear or to any other minutiae of rules,
but to the core principles around which we need to build our
lives. In other words, rather than calling them 'The Beatitudes',
we could quite rightly think of them as 'The BE-Attitudes'. After
all, they are about the attitudes that determine how we should *be*
during our lives on earth.

Because each beatitude fits with the others, they provide a
coherent description of what Jesus' followers are to be like. An
implication of this, of course, is that we cannot opt out of any
single beatitude. For example, we can't say, 'I believe in the
Beatitudes. I just don't do hungering and thirsting for righteousness', or 'I prefer to pass on all that meekness stuff.'

THE FUNCTION OF THE BEATITUDES

What was Jesus trying to achieve when He gave the Sermon on the Mount? What did He imagine the lasting effect of the Beatitudes would be?

They draw us to Jesus

By offering us challenges through quizzical, provocative statements, Jesus draws us to Himself. He makes His hearers think, helping us to understand more deeply the nature of the commitment and lifestyle He requests from His followers. Like the first people who heard these teachings, we are surprised and intrigued by them. As we learn from the disciple John's record of events, people who had been spying on Jesus went back to report to their seniors. Some interesting exchanges ensued: 'Finally the temple guards went back to the chief priests and Pharisees, who asked them, "Why didn't you bring him in?" "No one ever spoke the way this man does," the guards declared' (John 7:45–46). In other words, the guards were intrigued and also clearly sensed the authority of Jesus' words.

Even if no one has ever come away from reading the Beatitudes with a sense of having fully understood them, the extraordinary reality is that despite their profound and challenging morality Jesus actually lived them out Himself. He is a marvellous example of what they mean in practice. Jesus embodied the beatific life. He was meek and never put Himself first. He shunned the mighty and spent time with the poor. He was the great peacemaker, the one who spoke of peace, and the one who declared how men and women should make peace with God. He is also a wonderful example of someone who hungered and thirsted for righteousness because His focus was always on God His Father and on doing His Father's will. And of course, as for being persecuted for righteousness, He experienced this in its fullness. It was not just that the cross was an appalling punishment; it was that He, of all people, was totally innocent.

When we realise the challenge of living out the Beatitudes, we're likely to be even more drawn to Jesus' teachings, recognising Him as the person He implicitly claimed to be, God in the form of man.

They condemn us

On a less uplifting note, it is also true to say that the Beatitudes condemn us. Let me suggest that you treat them as categories on a scorecard for us to measure our worth. If you had to give yourself an honest score of 0 to 3 for each one, what would your overall score be? Let's say: 0 means, 'I don't fit this description at all', 1 means, 'I only rarely fit this description', 2 means, 'I sometimes fit this description' and 3 means, 'This description always fits me.' Read through these questions and try to give yourself an honest score.

Starting at the end and going backwards

Are you at all likely to be persecuted because of righteousness? Are you such an influence for good that those who are corrupt, or do wrong, actually see you as a threat? Or are you of so little importance that they don't even know who you are?

Are you a peacemaker? Do you like to restore that which is broken? Does it bring you joy to see another person brought to a state of knowing forgiveness? Or do you actually find squabbles really rather useful because you can use them for your own ends?

Are you pure in heart? Do you have utter integrity? Or do you like playing games with people? Are you truly honest? Or are you a play actor? Do you put on a façade at church and at work, and possibly even before God when you pray in private at home?

Could your actions be described as merciful or even kind? Or are you tough? A verbal bruiser? Do you empathise with others? Do people come up to you and say: 'I have a problem. Can you help me?' Do you grieve over suffering or do you coldly walk past?

Is your greatest desire and deepest passion to hunger and thirst for what is right? Or do you put your own desires and yourself first? Does your life revolve around your own status, prosperity and pleasure?

Are you meek? Or do you actually think you're better than other people? Do you flaunt yourself and throw your weight around, so as to make sure people know exactly who you are? Do you want people to think that you're actually pretty important?

It's a challenging list, isn't it? If you've been at all honest, by the time you have got this far in the list of beatitudes, you may feel rather disappointed with yourself. On the bright side, that's exactly the kind of state of mind the first two beatitudes require.

Do you really mourn over the state of your moral life? Are you glib or shallow when it comes to morality? Do you grieve over your sinfulness?

Are you poor in spirit? Or do you really think that you're actually not too bad? Do you realise you'll never be able to impress God with your actions? Do you understand that it is by His grace alone that you can be accepted and welcomed into the kingdom?

I suspect your score sheet, like mine, is looking pretty miserable. Is it only on the first and second beatitudes that you can give yourself a good score? When Jesus gave the Beatitudes, He probably intended to force us back to basics so that we realise that we've fallen short of God's standards. Their purpose is to make us repent.

They comfort us

If you do indeed find yourself sitting there with a miserable score sheet, the Beatitudes then have another interesting effect: they somehow manage to comfort us too! Having done a bit of self-examination you're prepared to admit that you've failed on all the Beatitudes. I can imagine that a thought crosses your mind: 'Hey! Wouldn't it be nice if I could somehow have Jesus' perfect score?' Now, if you know anything about modern-day examinations you know that identity fraud is a major concern. Is the student sitting the exam the person he or she actually claims to be? Of course, that kind of identity fraud is both immoral and illegal but I can imagine, if you're at all human, you might think it tempting to somehow swap test papers with Jesus. What's really amazing about Christianity is that Jesus allows us to do just this. The message of the New Testament is that we exchange our failed and inadequate righteousness for Jesus' perfect righteousness. In return He takes our sin and pays for it on the cross. An extraordinary transfer is offered: His righteousness for our sin.

Paul summarises this idea in a letter to the Philippians:

> What is more, I consider everything a loss compared to the surpassing greatness of knowing Christ Jesus my Lord, for whose sake I have lost all things. I consider them rubbish, that I may gain Christ and be found in him, *not having a righteousness of my own that comes from the law, but that which is through faith in Christ – the righteousness that comes from God and is by faith.* (Philippians 3:8–9; emphasis mine)

Peter also said it well: 'For Christ died for sins once for all, the righteous for the unrighteous, to bring you to God' (1 Peter 3:18).

They point us towards happiness

The Beatitudes mark out the road to a happy state of mind and existence. Through these eight short statements, Jesus promises us that if we seek to be blessed and to be a blessing, we will know deeper happiness and satisfaction than anything else this life can offer us. It's a pretty good deal, don't you think?